COW CORNER

VIKRAM VALLURI

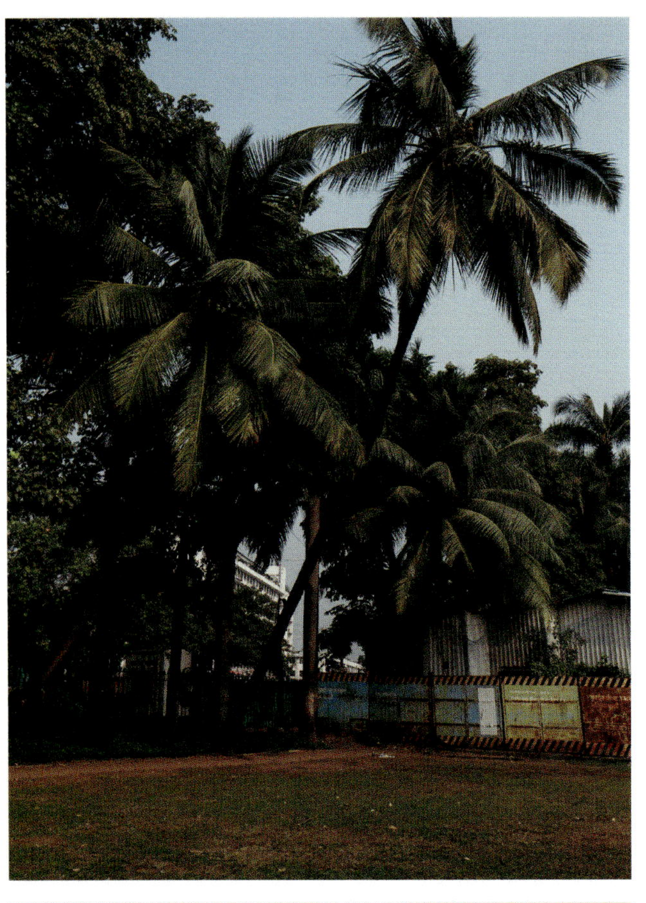
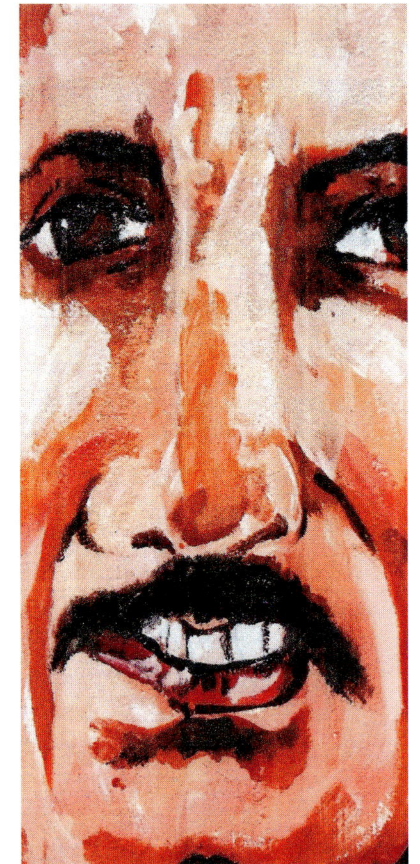
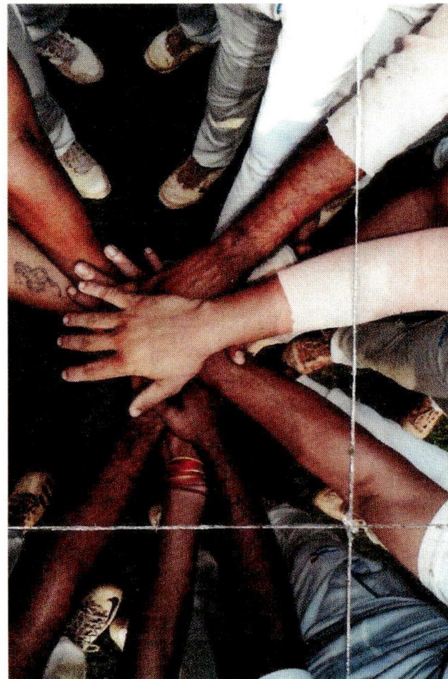
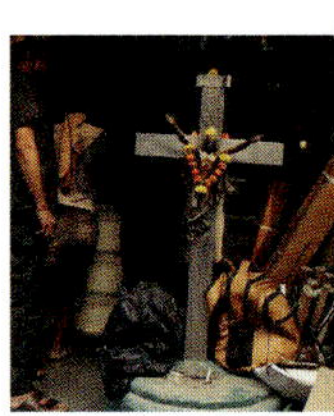
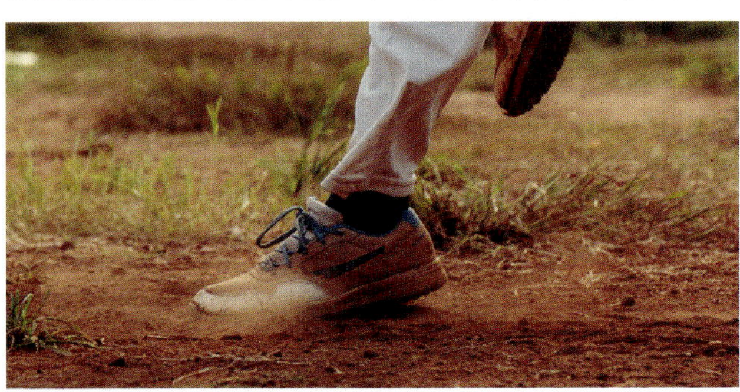
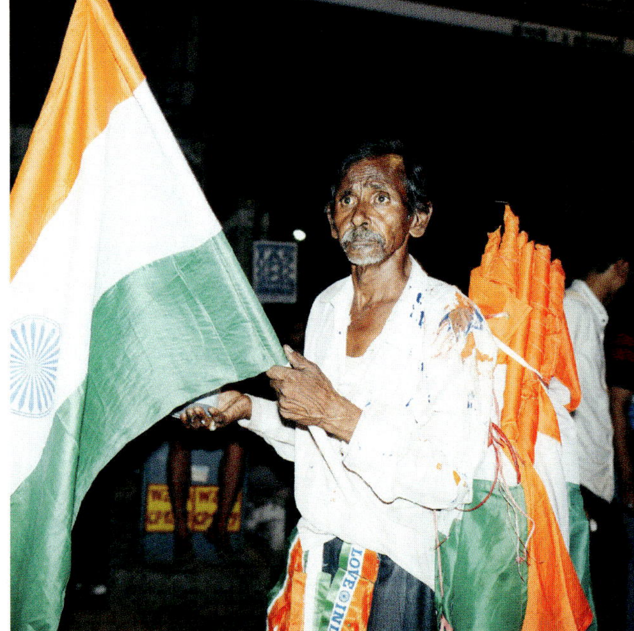
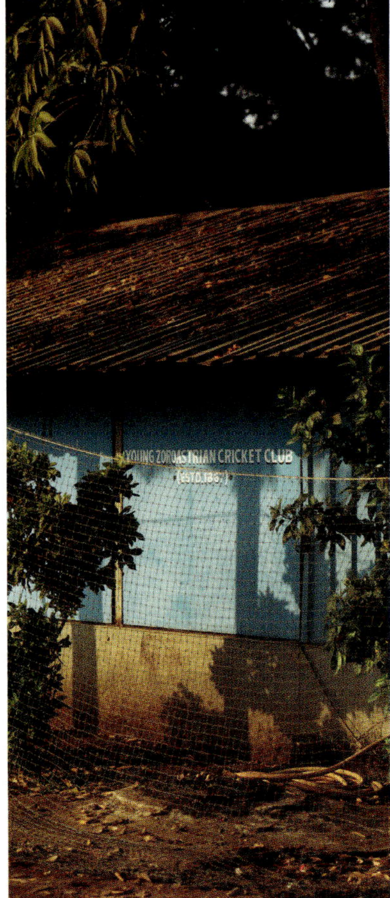
YOUNG ZOROASTRIAN CRICKET CLUB
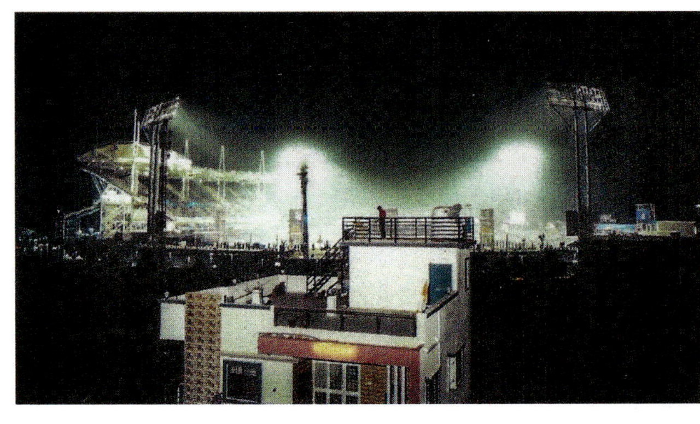
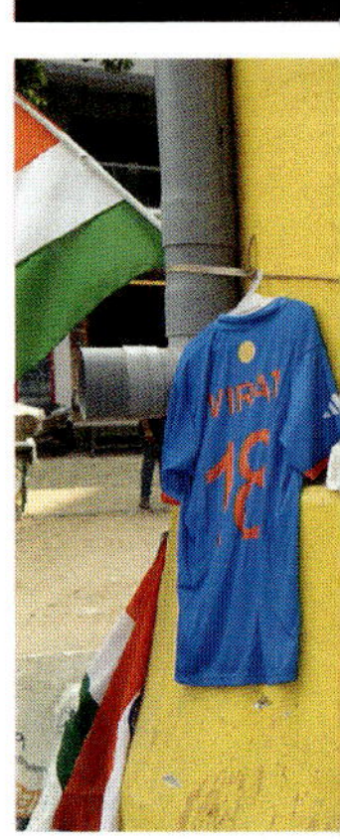

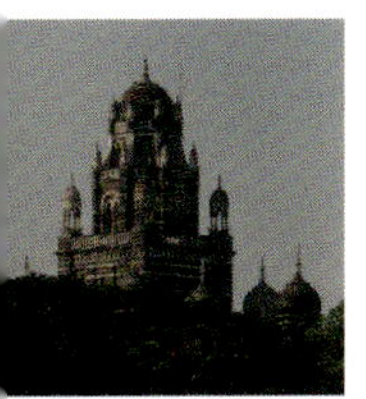

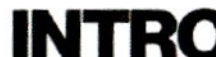

INTRO

India, a land of evolving transformations, has beckoned me year after year, compelling me to preserve and keep pace with its ever-changing landscape.

After publishing my Zine, Keep Calm and Carry On, documenting the One Day International Cricket World Cup (ICC World Cup) in 2019, I intend to continue my photographic journey with the ICC World Cup every four years.

COW CORNER

This ICC World Cup 2023 hosted by India holds special significance and relevance for Indians for whom cricket is more than just a sport. Cricket in India is often cast as religion amongst non-fans and fans who come together as one nation to vent frustration or anger, share sorrow or grief, indulge in discussions, or celebrate together, irrespective of one's socioeconomic, cultural, political, or religious differences.

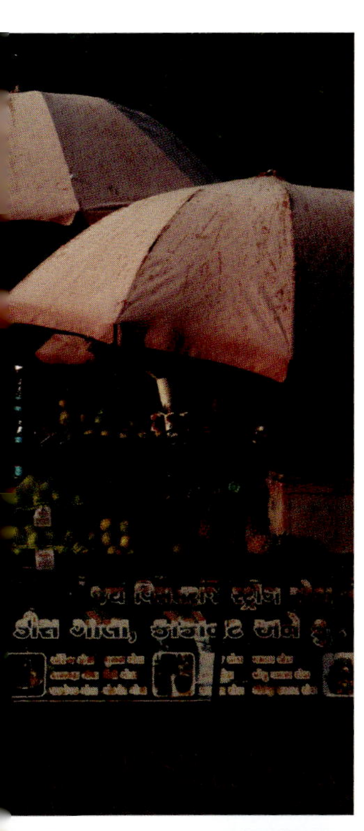

From October to November 2023, I crisscrossed Indian cities that hosted matches– Pune, Ahmedabad, Delhi, and Mumbai. Most people attended the games to watch cricket, while I recognized that cricket is more than just a stadium event. I saw firsthand how cricket permeated every facet of Indian life. Cricket in India is akin to a lifeforce, a heart pumping blood to India's arteries and veins and Indian life in its entirety, be it in arts, commerce, prayer, or more.

Watching the matches live and on television gave me a unique perspective as a player and a fan. My mission was to reveal how cricket is the underlying rhythm that keeps India enthralled in myriad forms. "Cow Corner" explores the essence of cricket's omnipresence in India's tapestry.

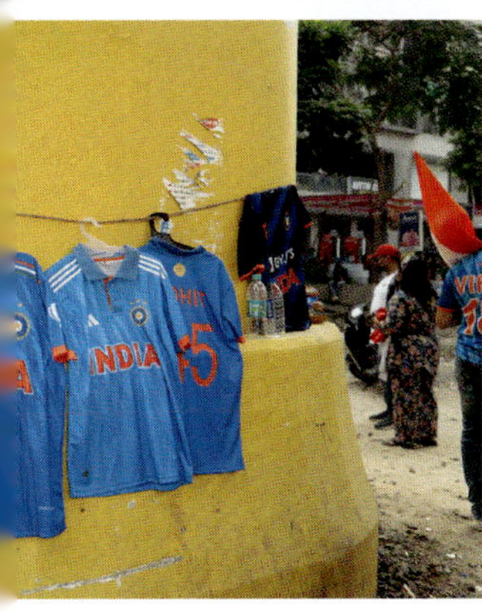

- VIKRAM VALLURI

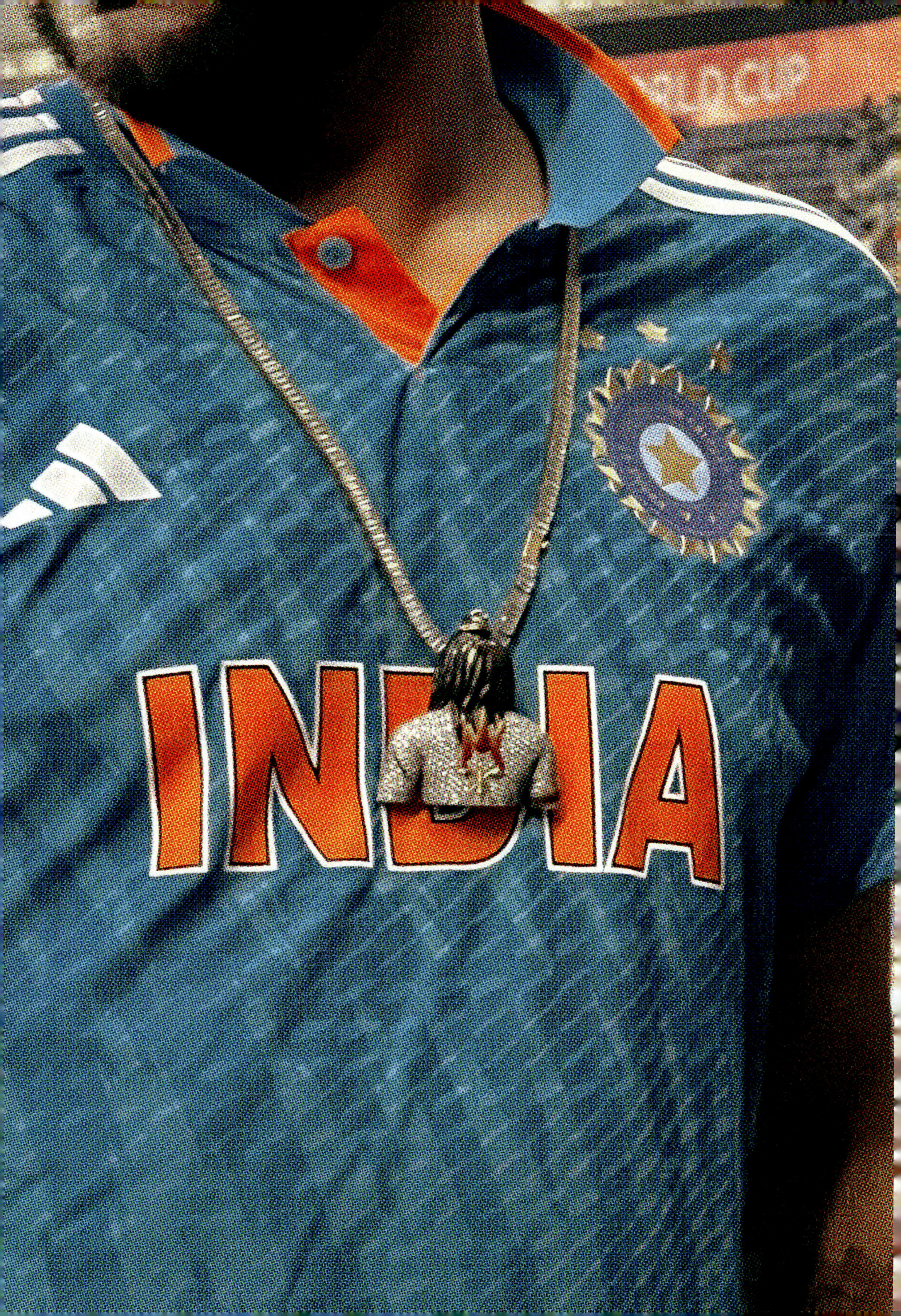
INDIA

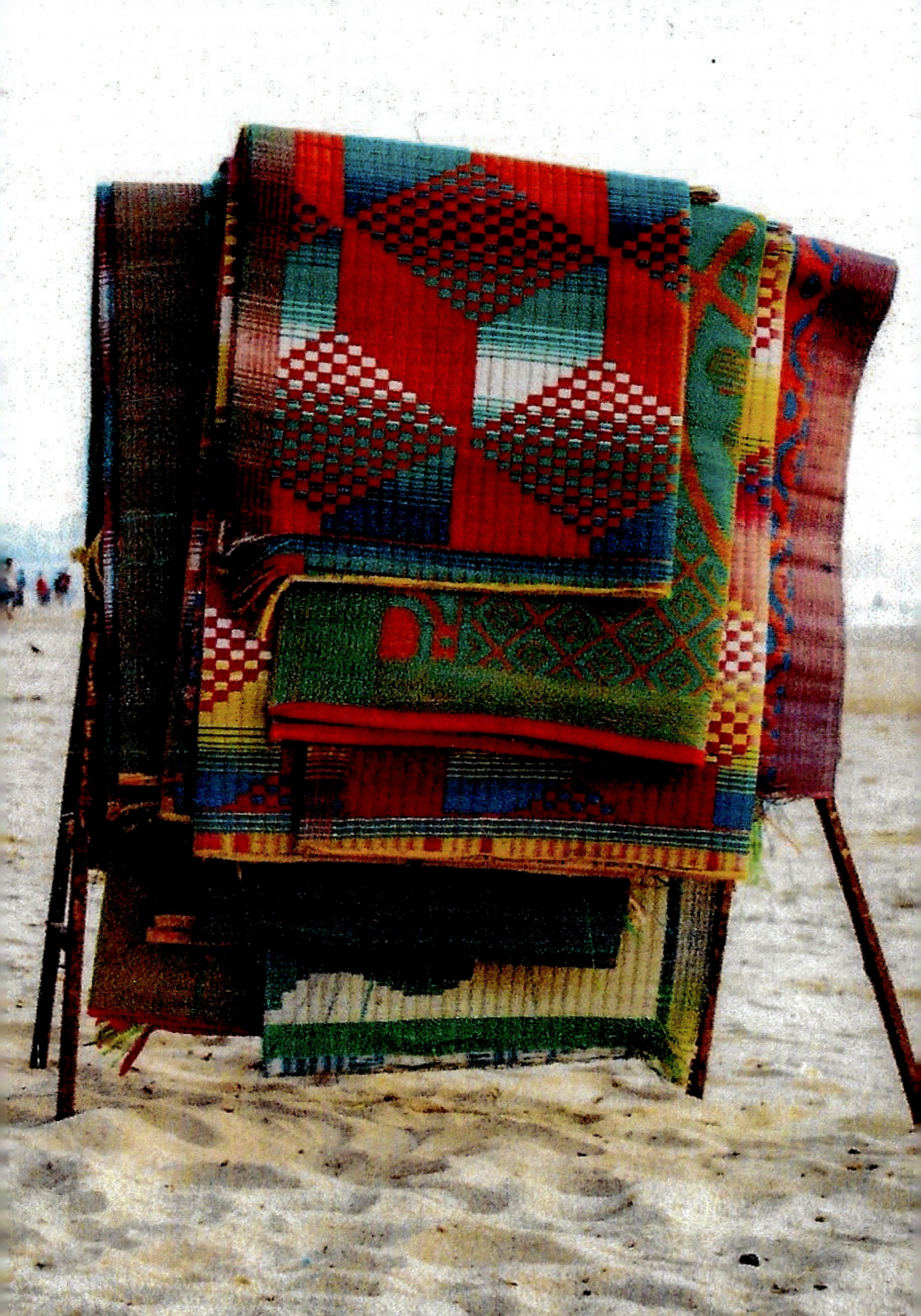

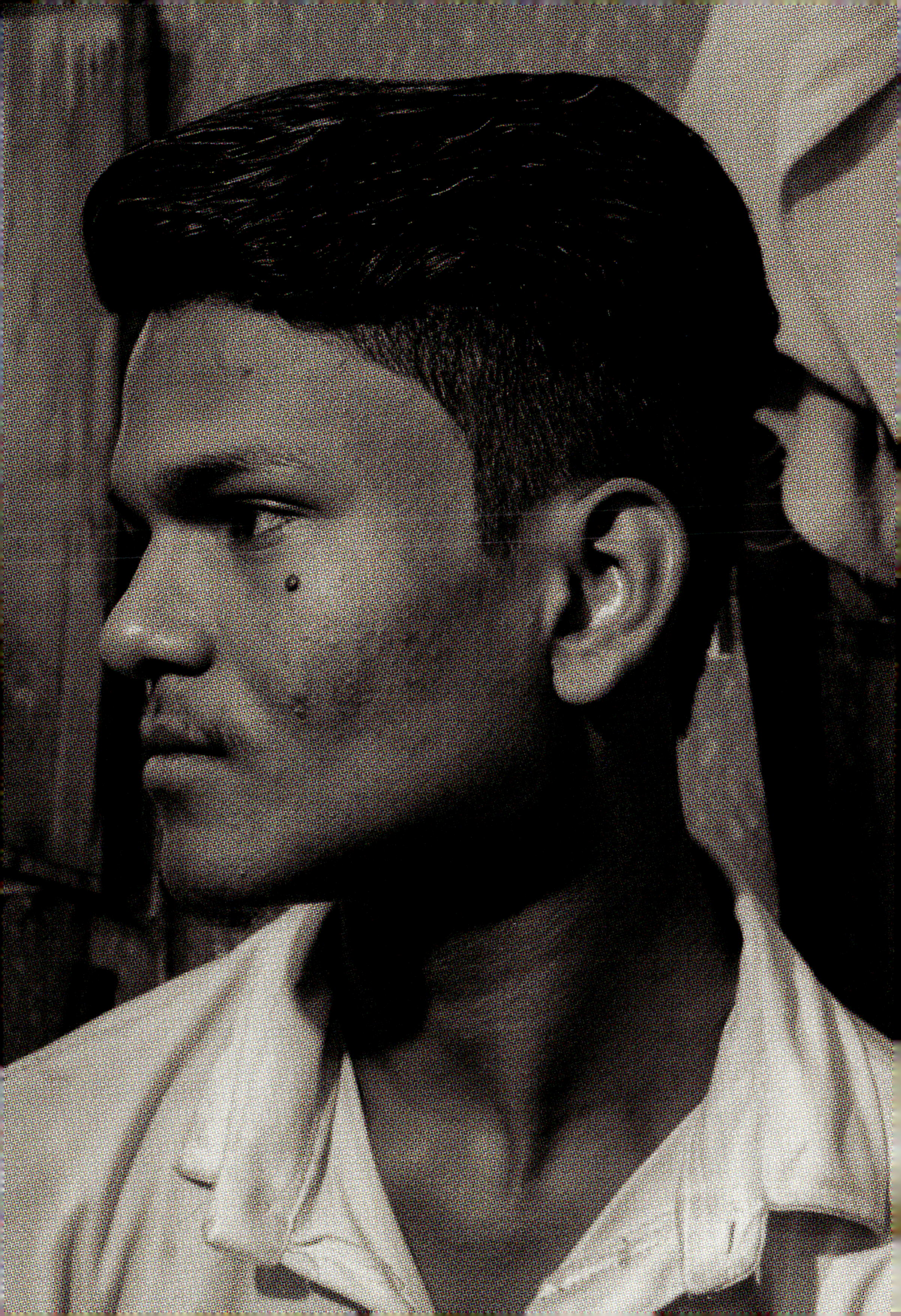

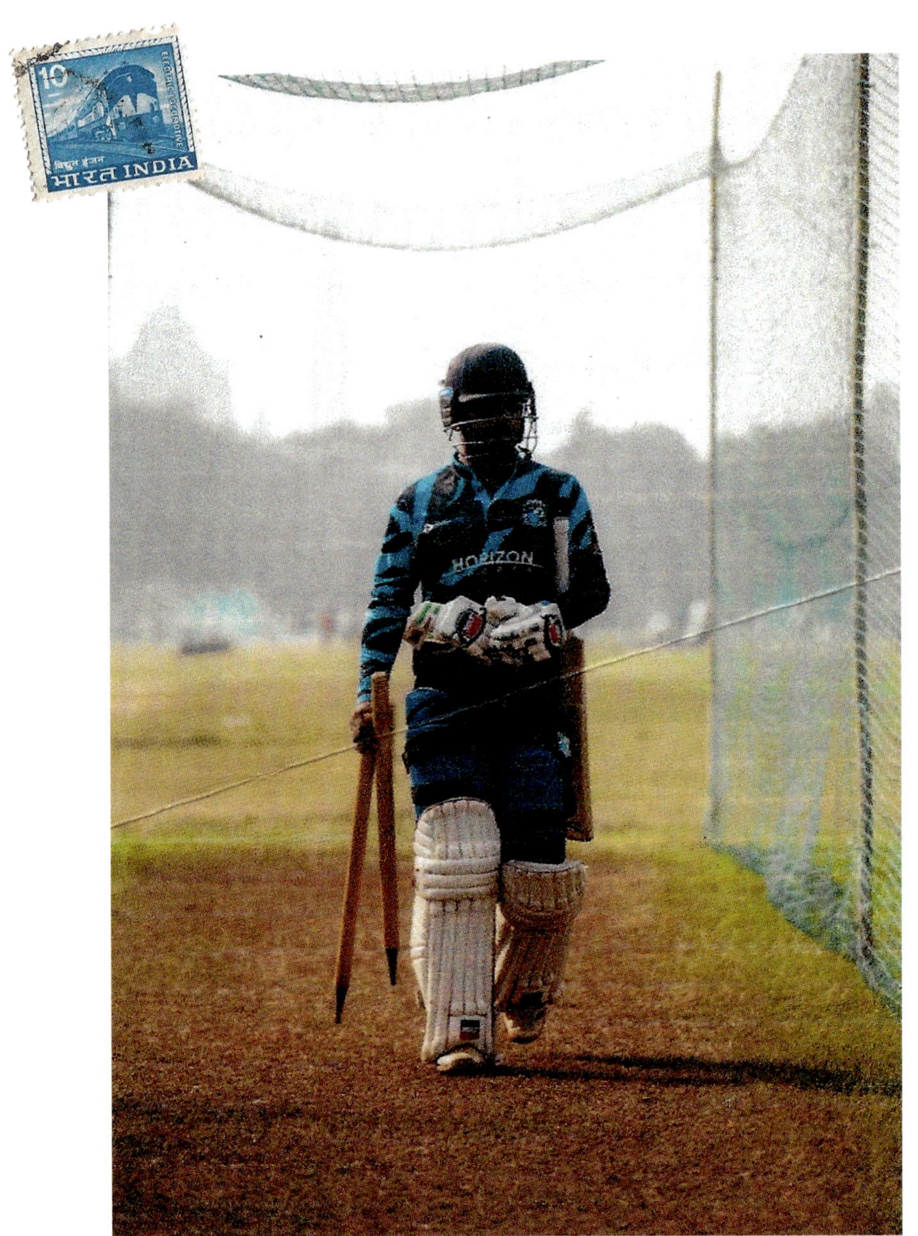
10
भारत INDIA
HORIZON

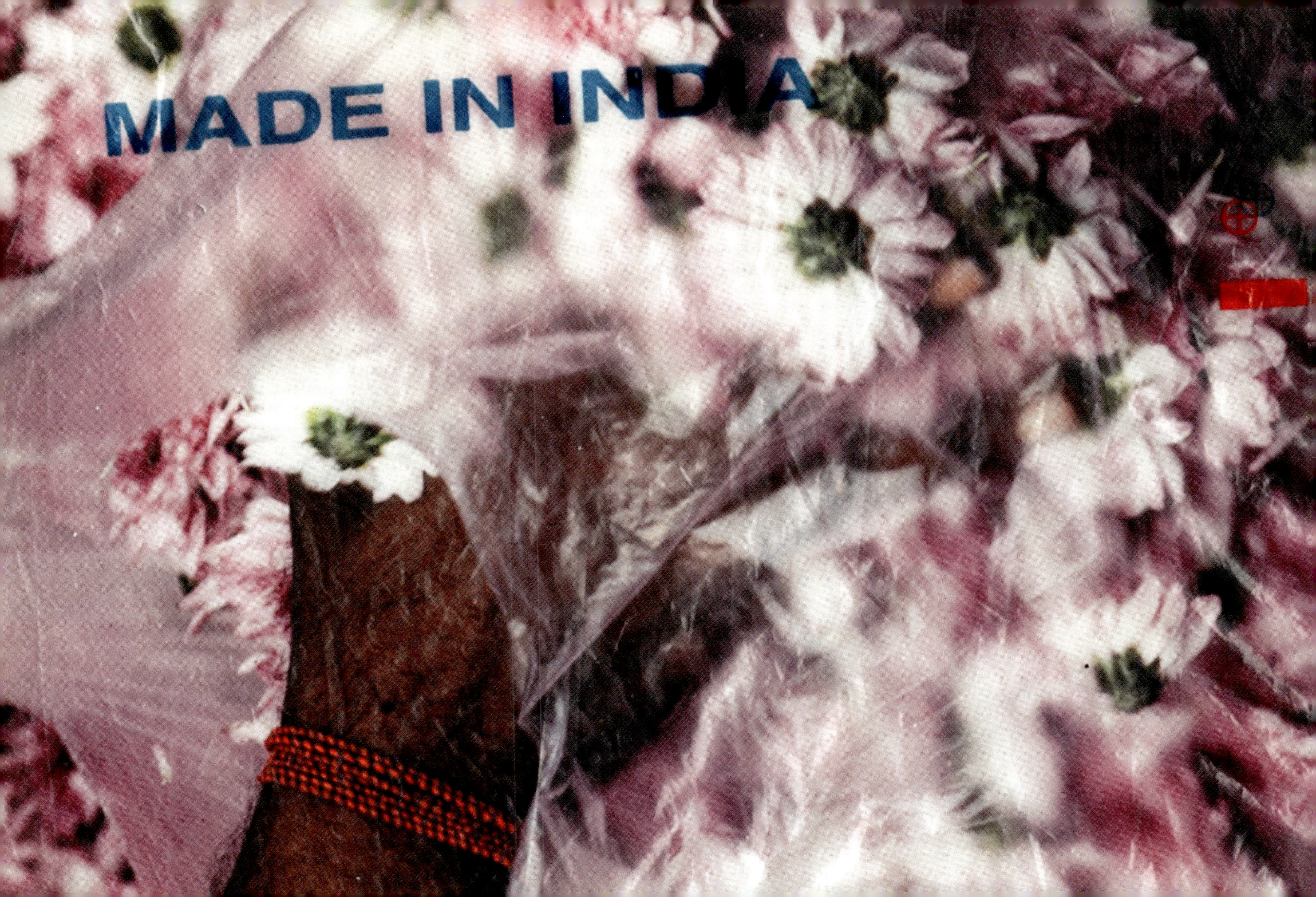
MADE IN INDIA

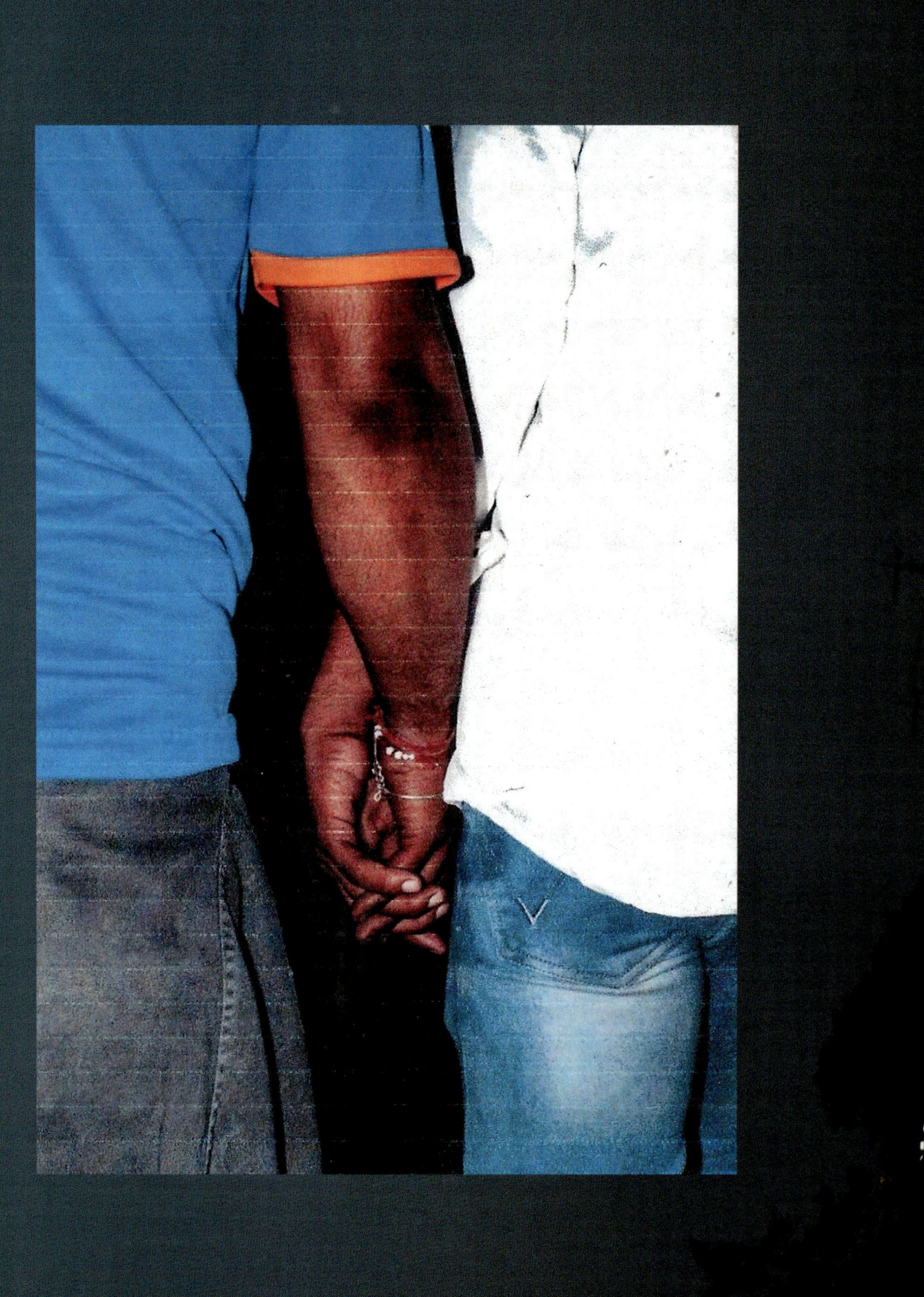

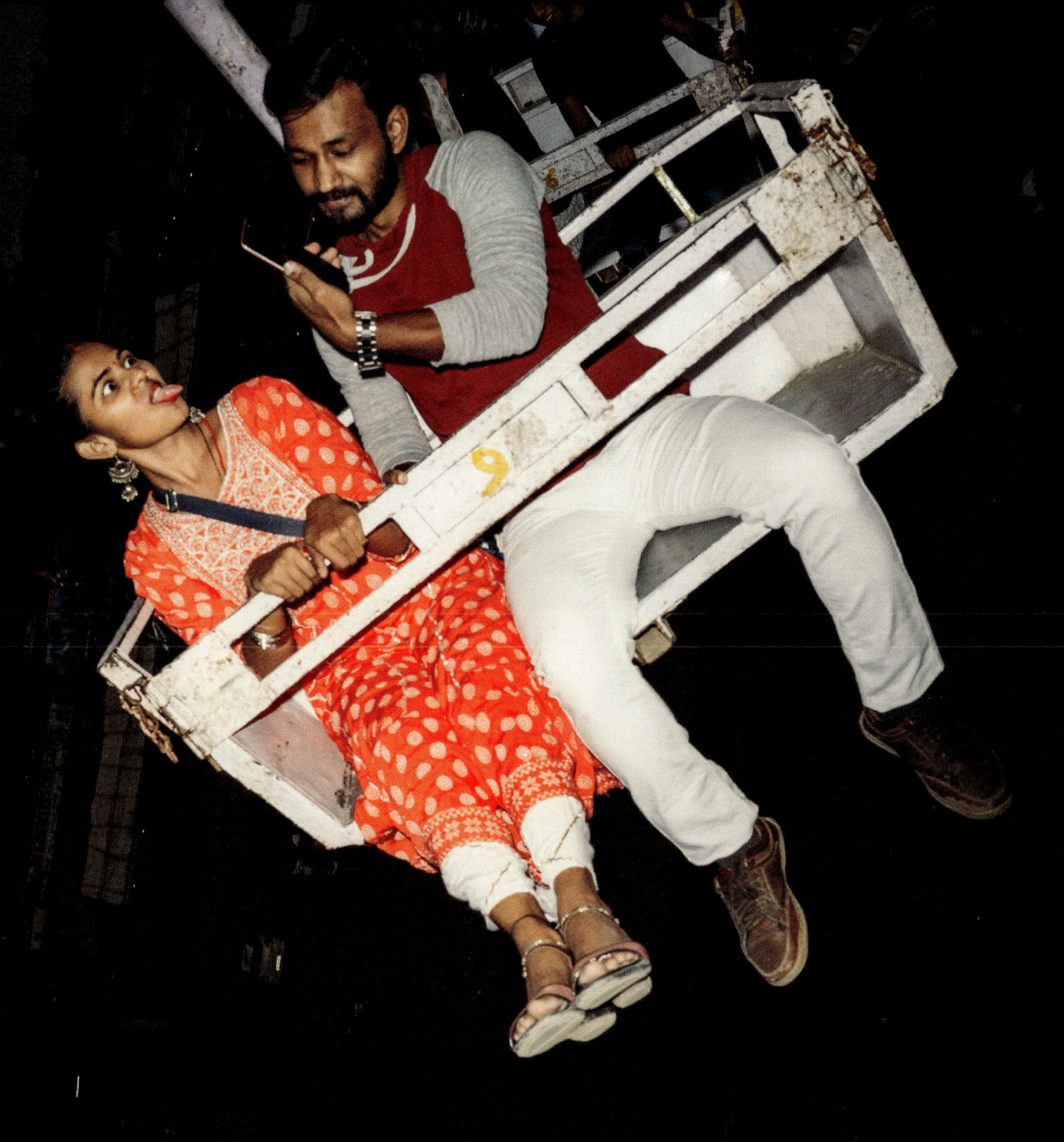

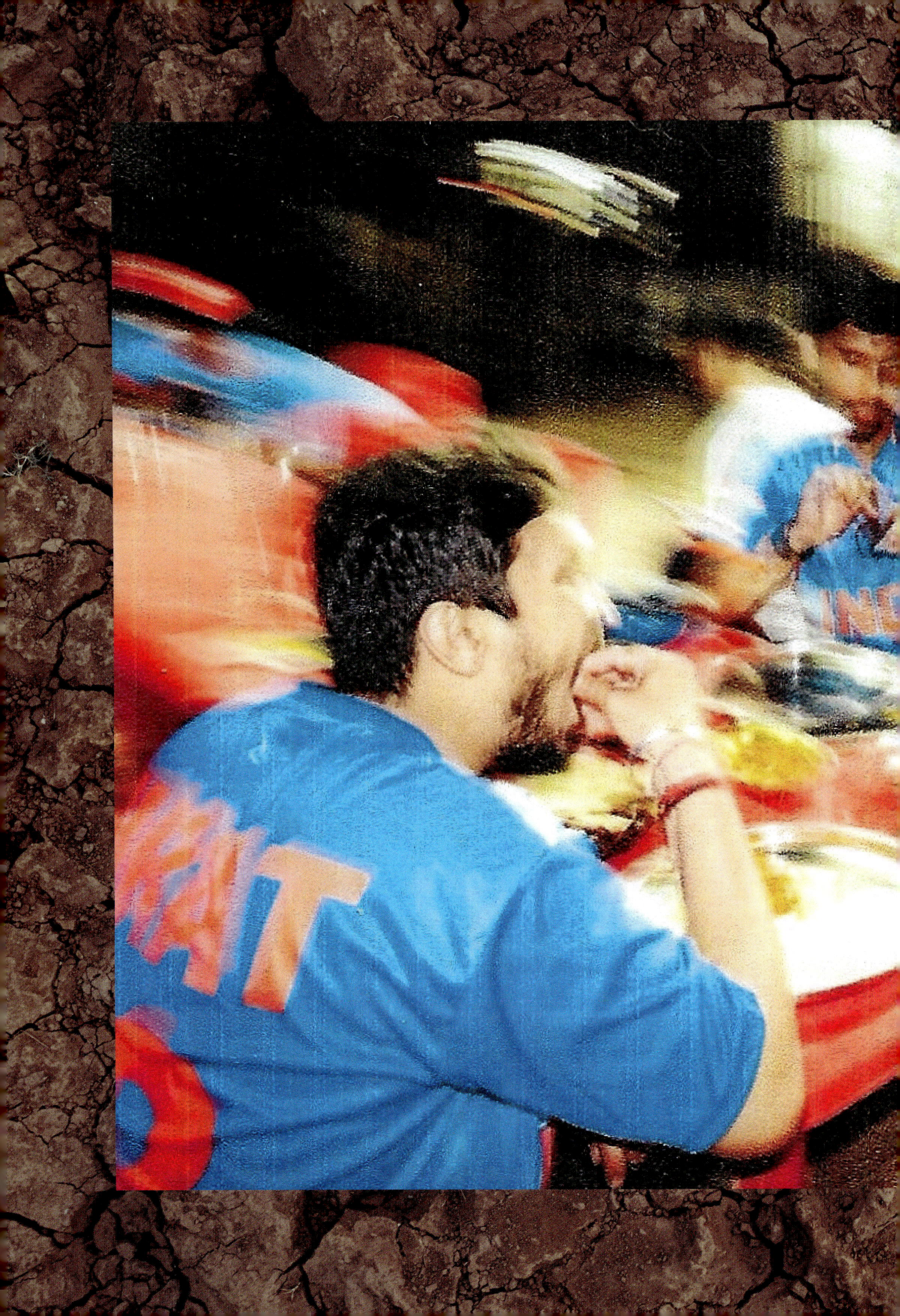

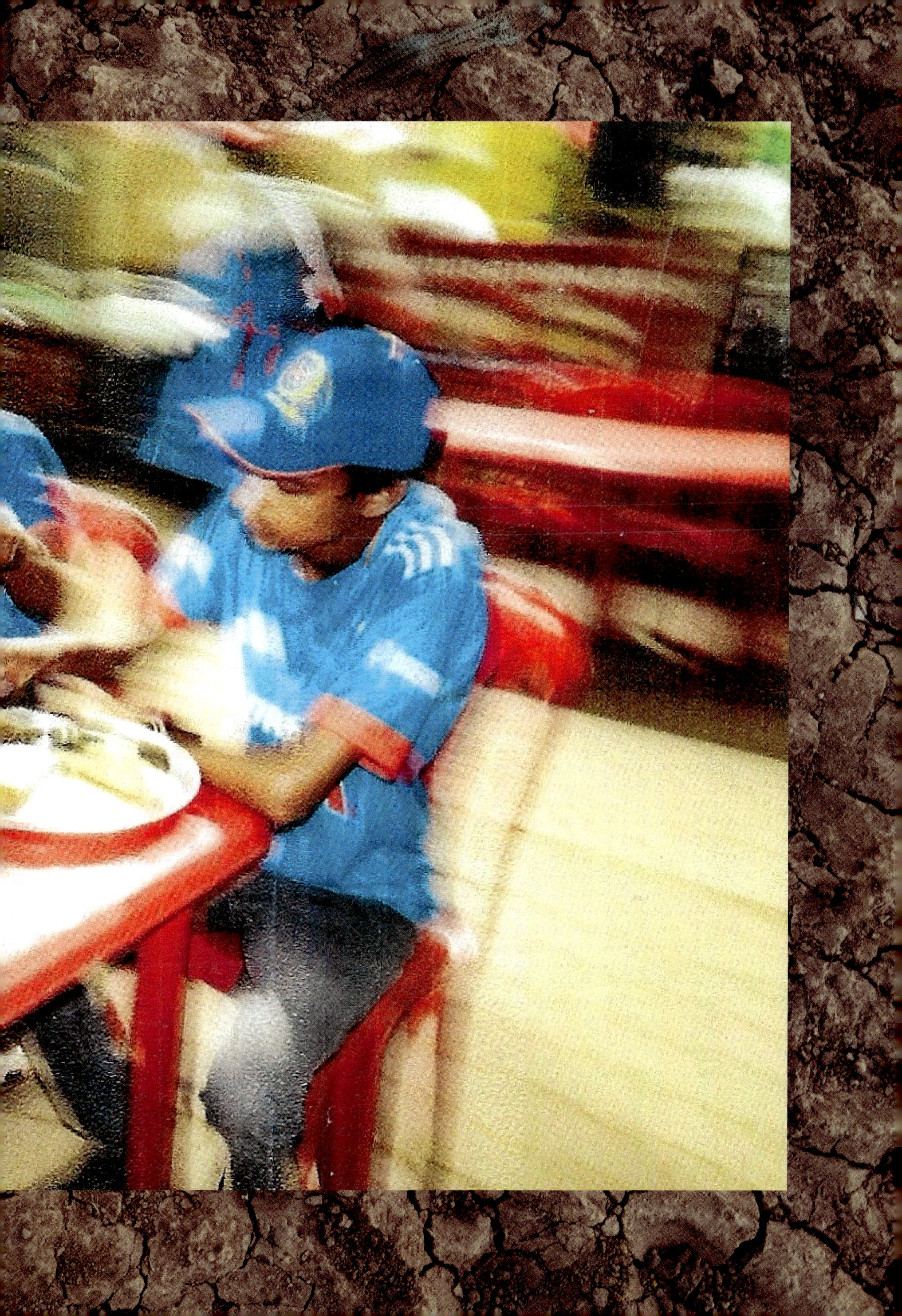

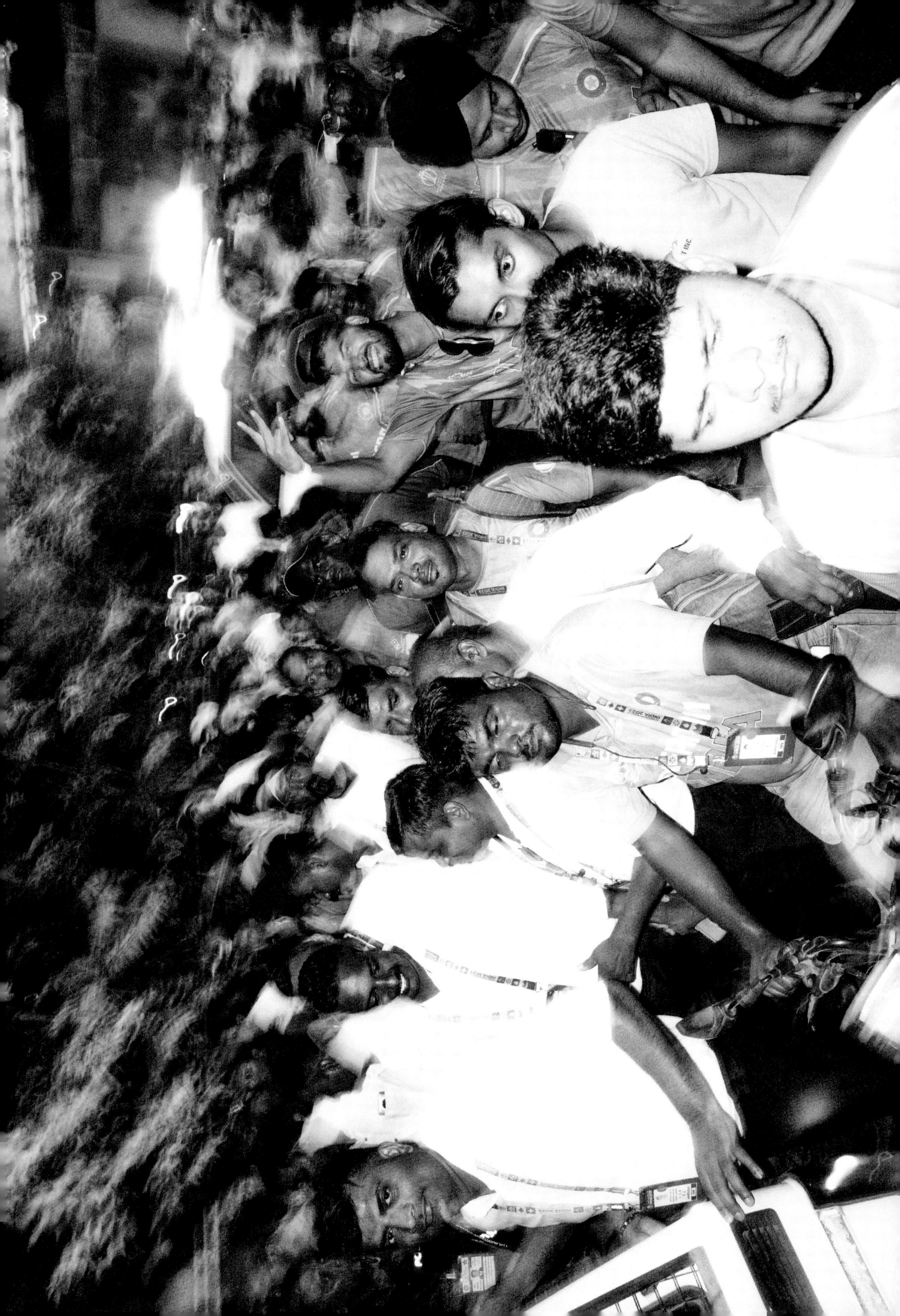

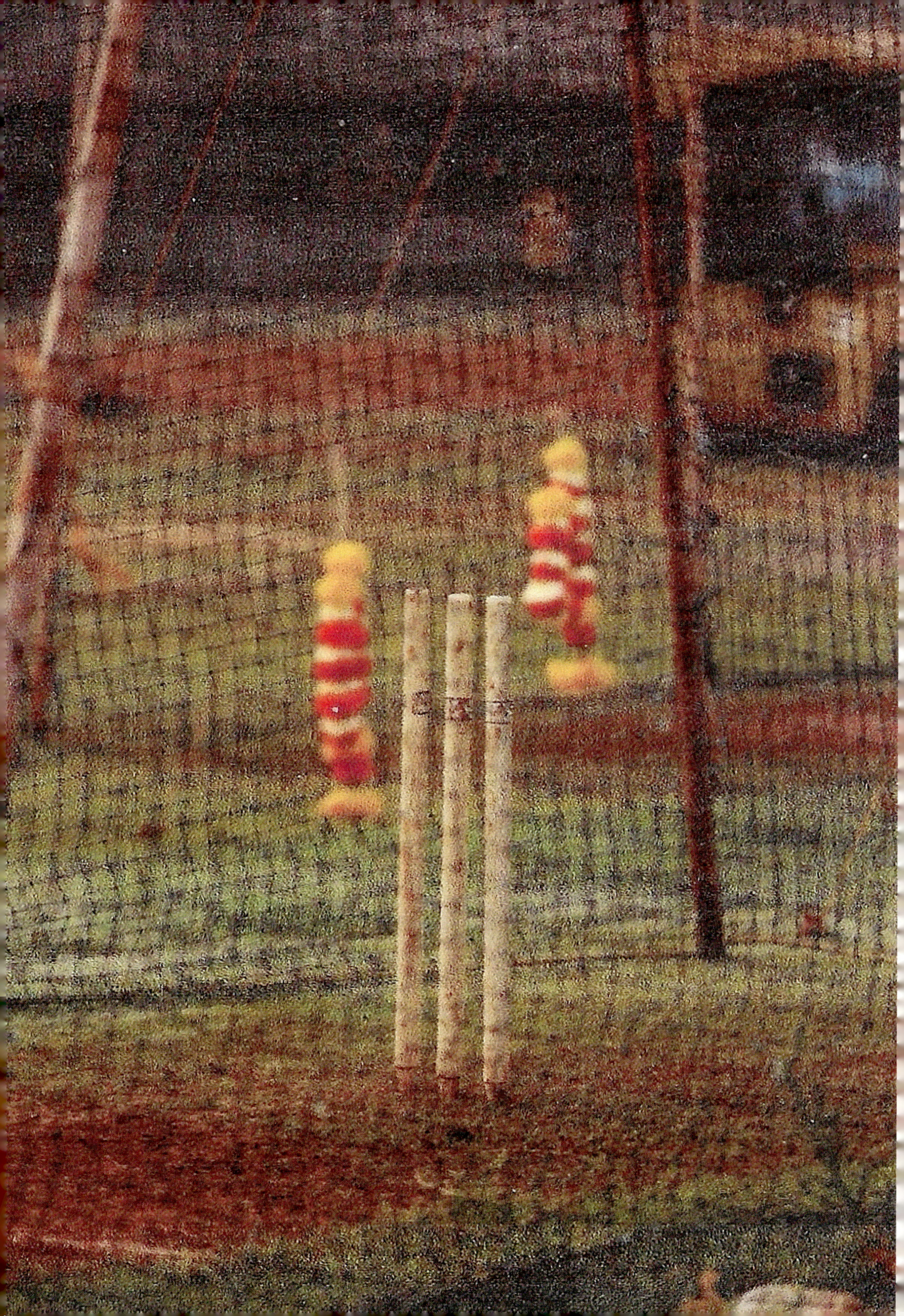

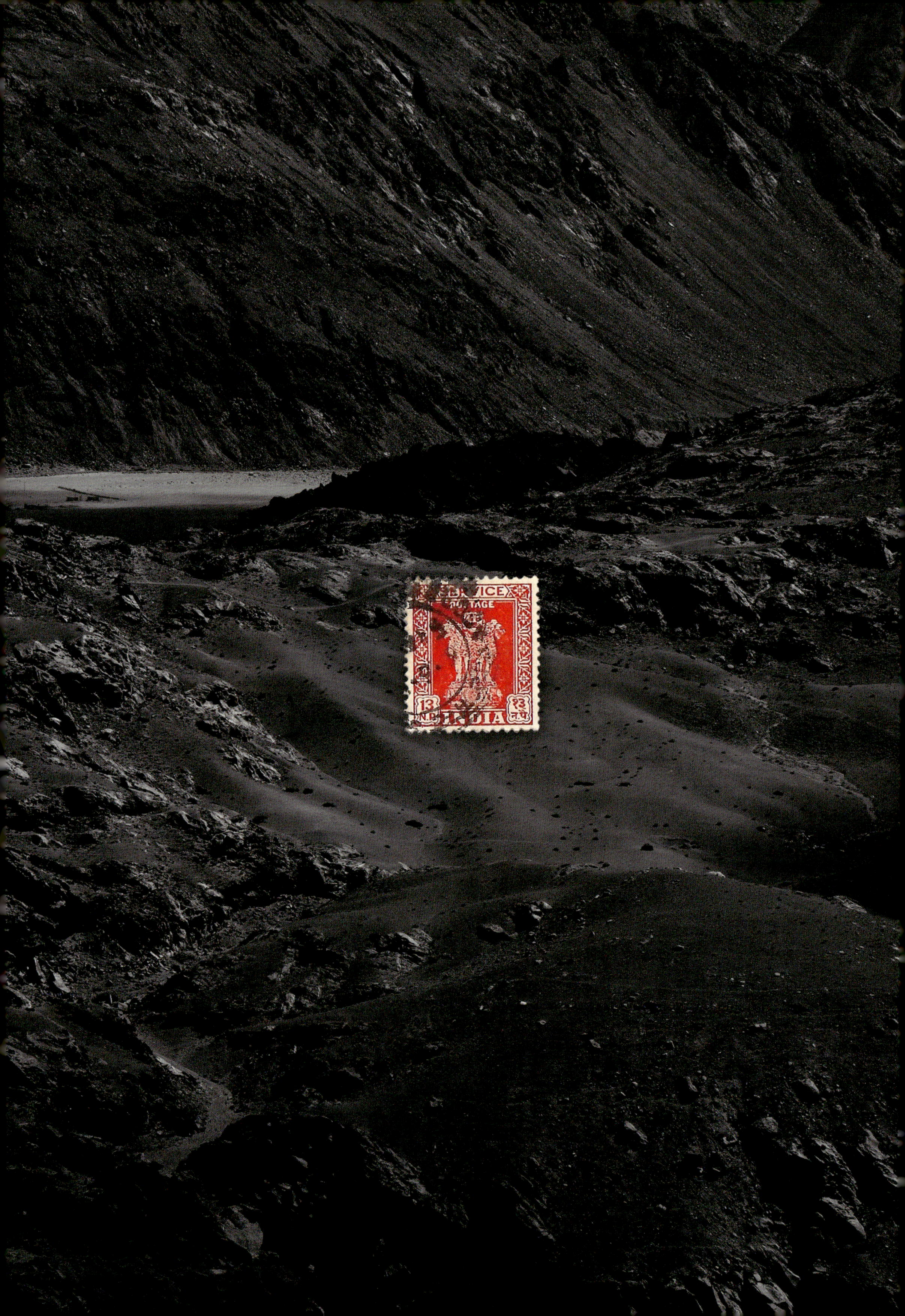
13
N.P.

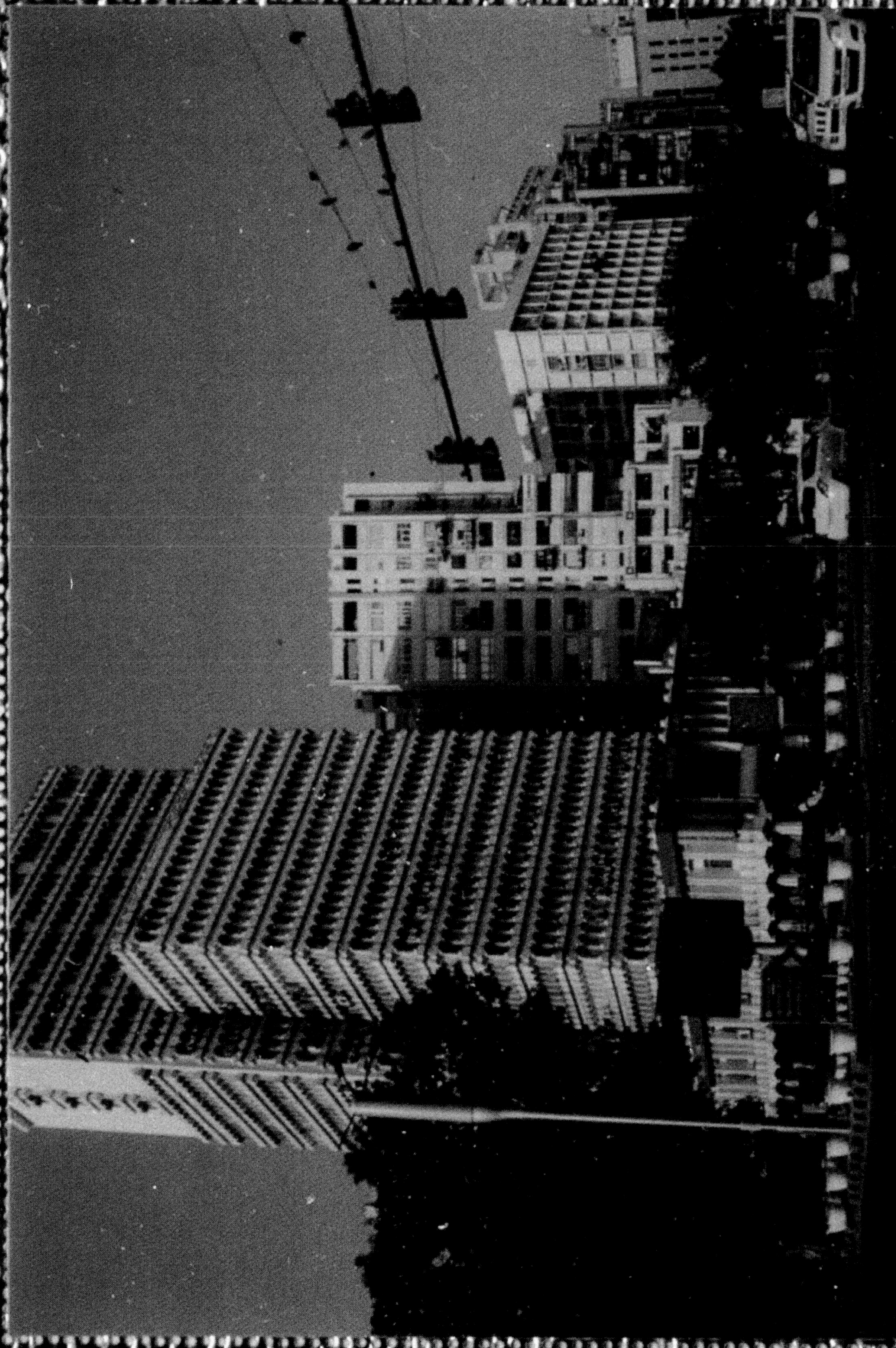

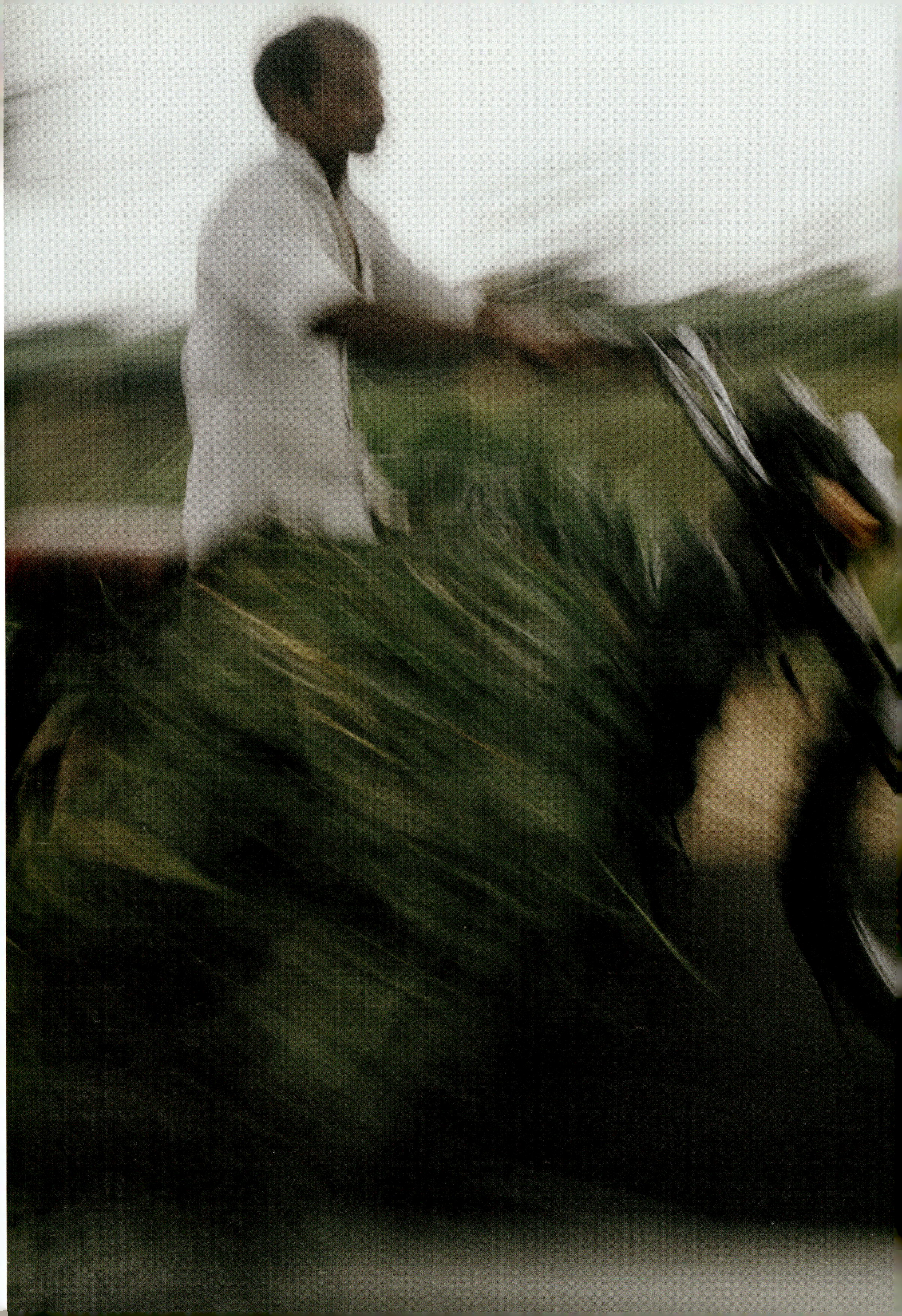

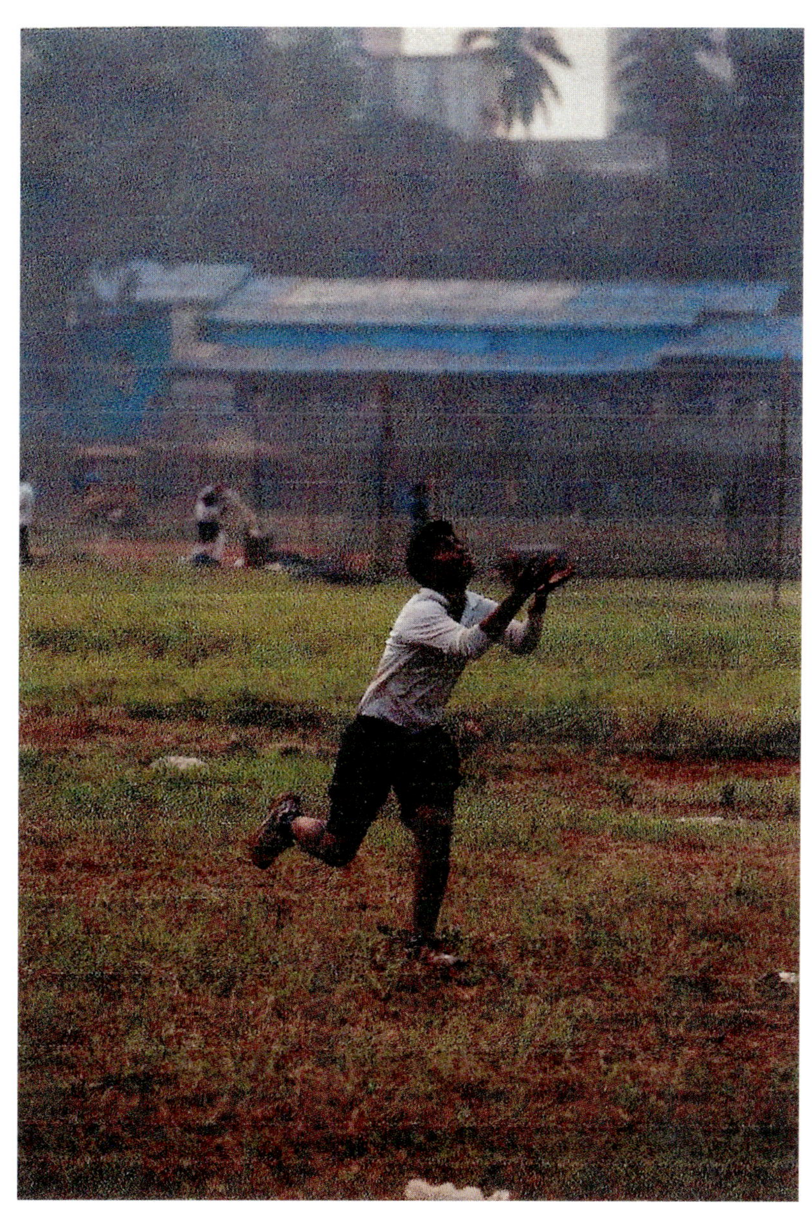

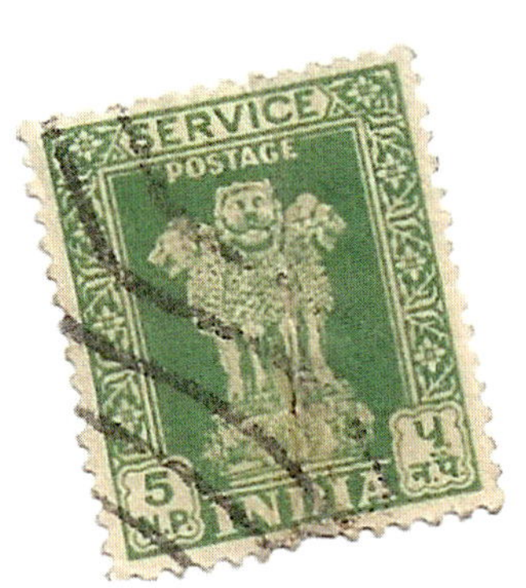
SERVICE
POSTAGE
5
N.P.
INDIA

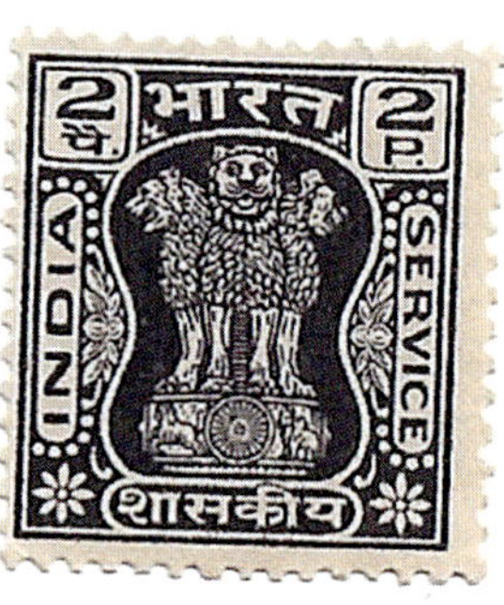
2
भारत
2
P.
INDIA
SERVICE
शासकीय

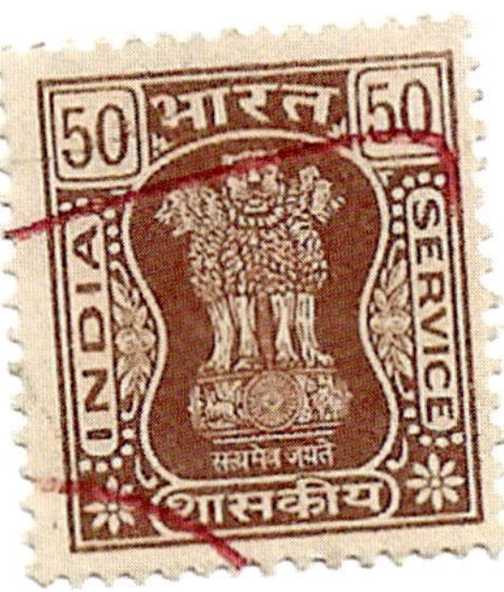
50
भारत
50
INDIA
SERVICE
सत्यमेव जयते
शासकीय

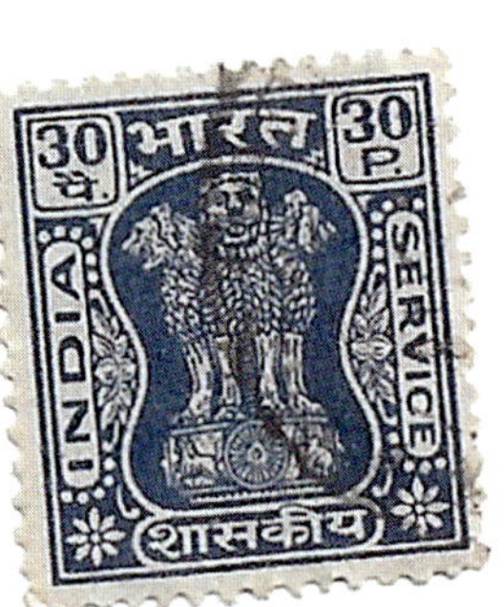
30
भारत
30
P.
INDIA
SERVICE
शासकीय

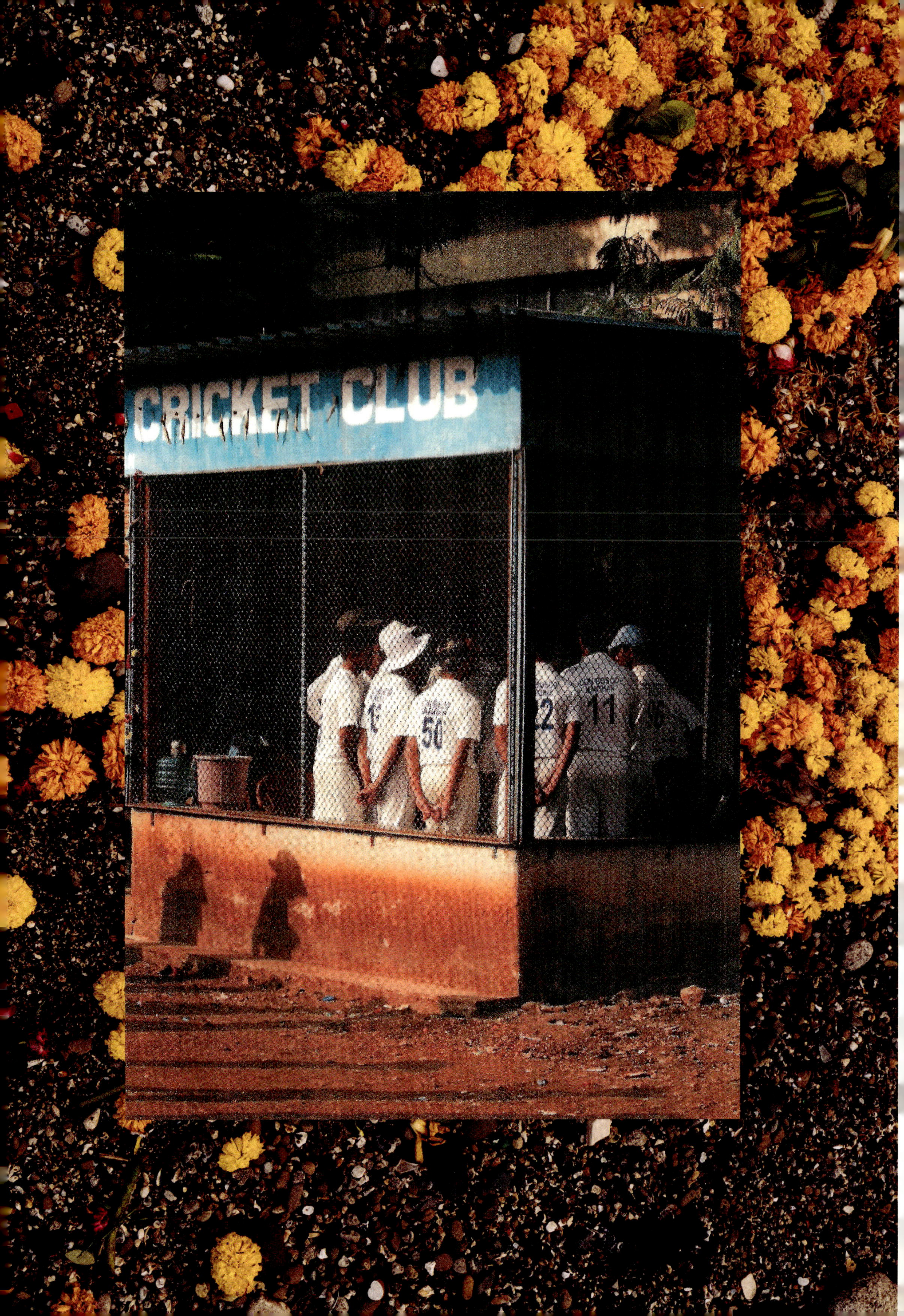
CRICKET CLUB

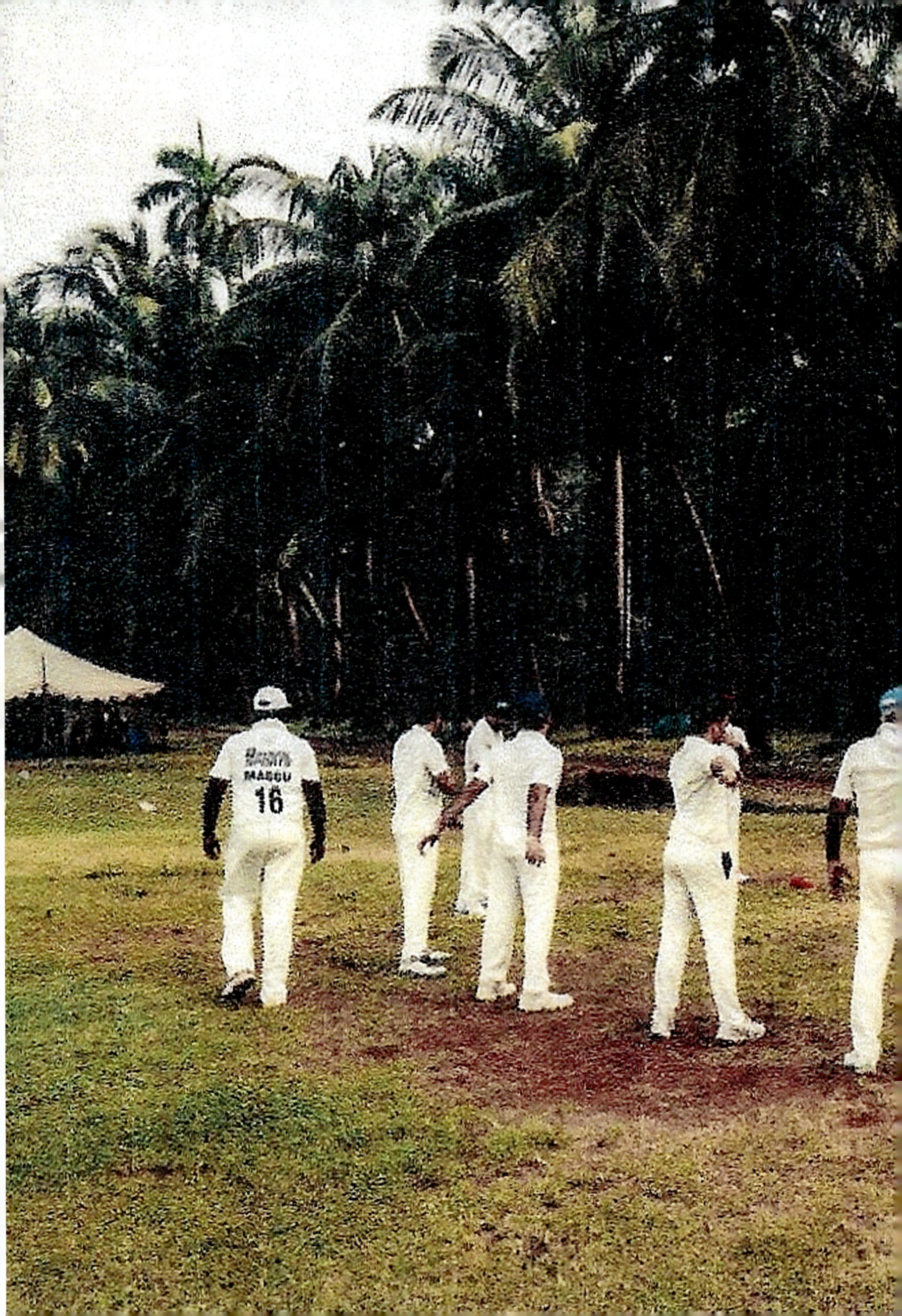
16

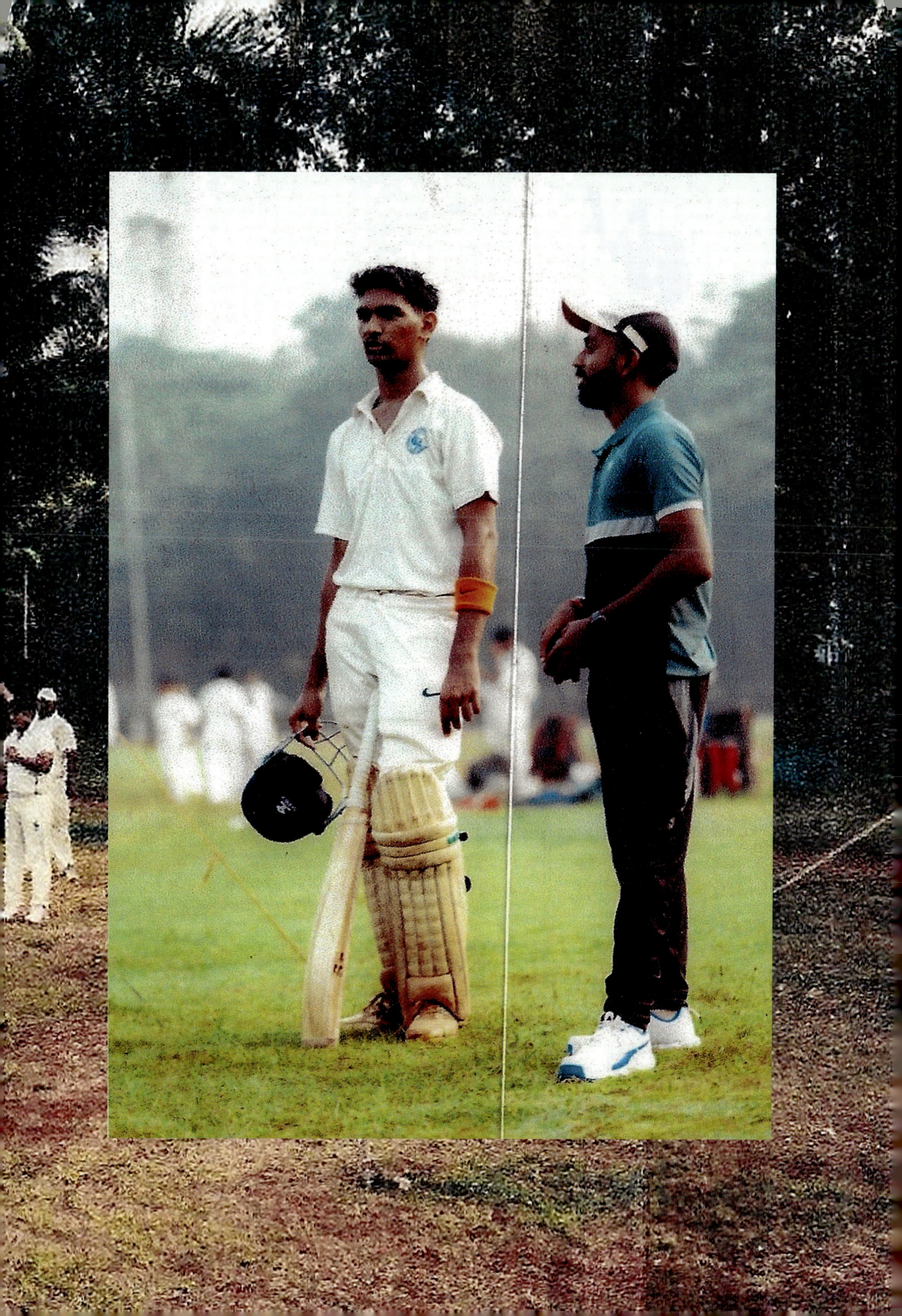

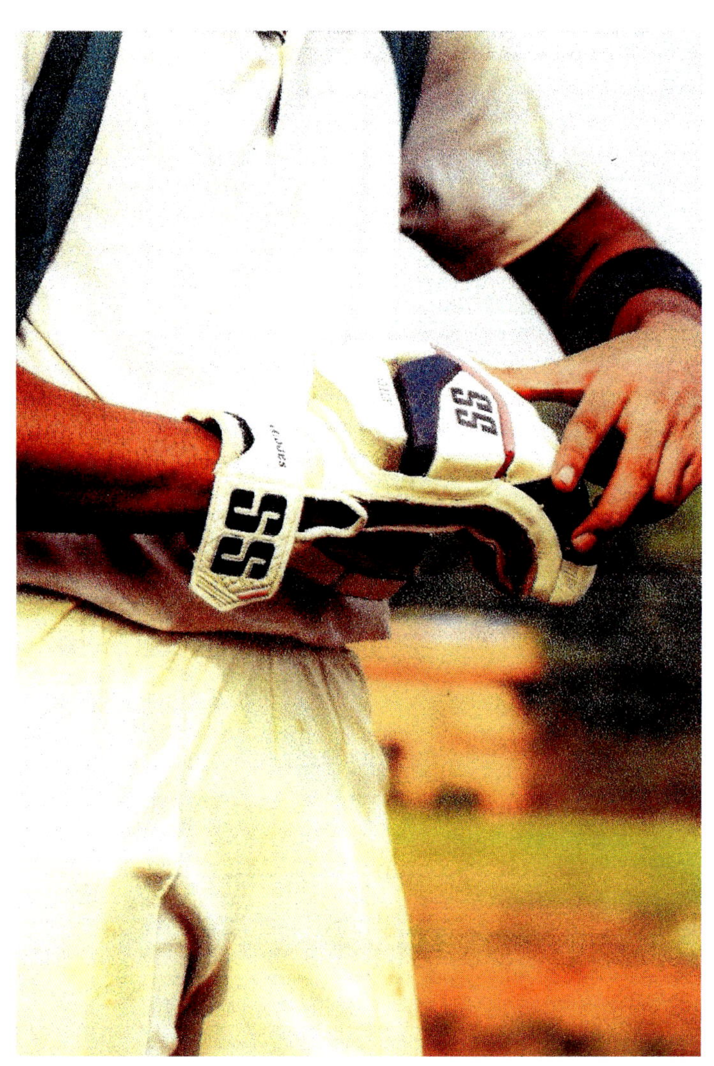
SS
SS

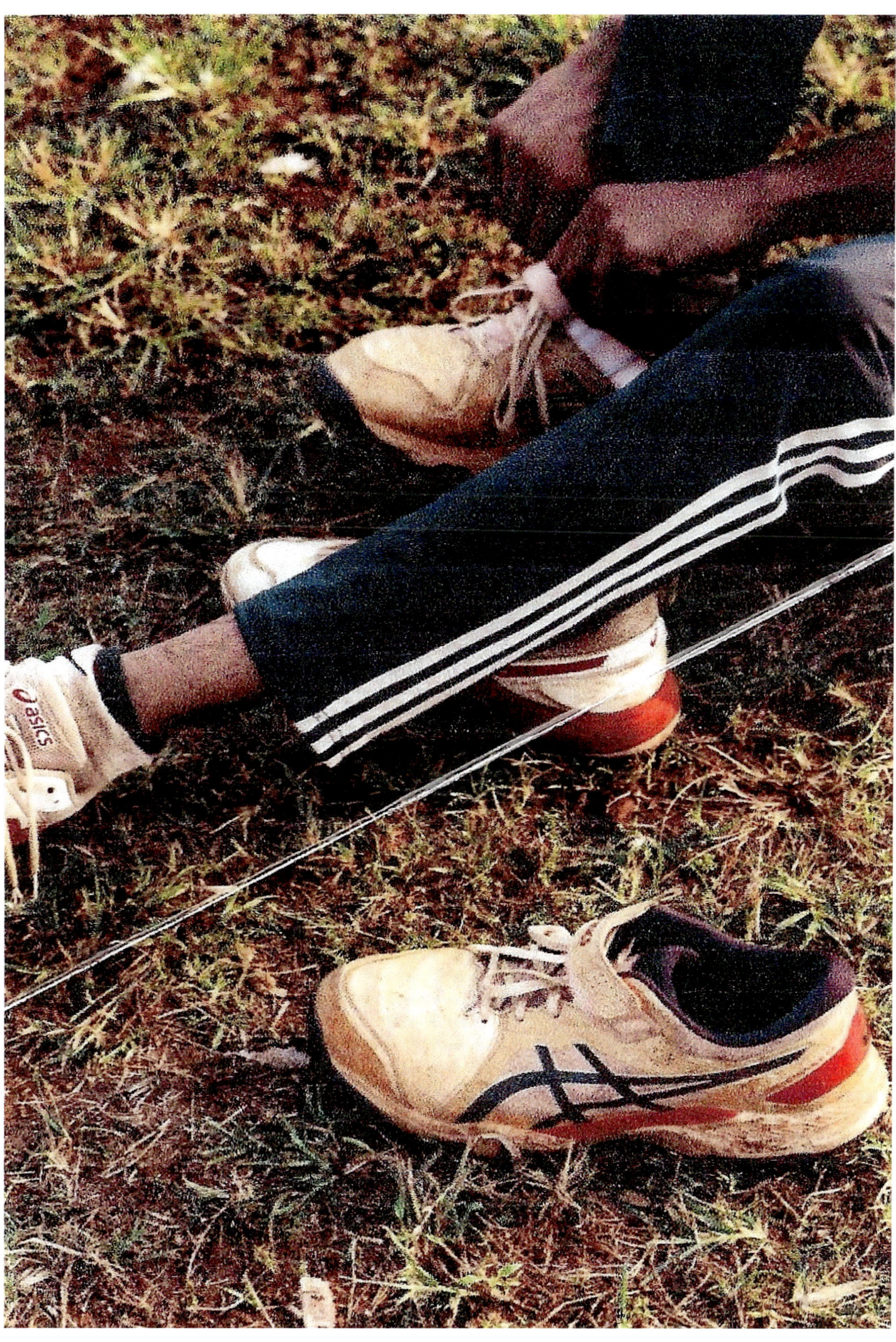
asics

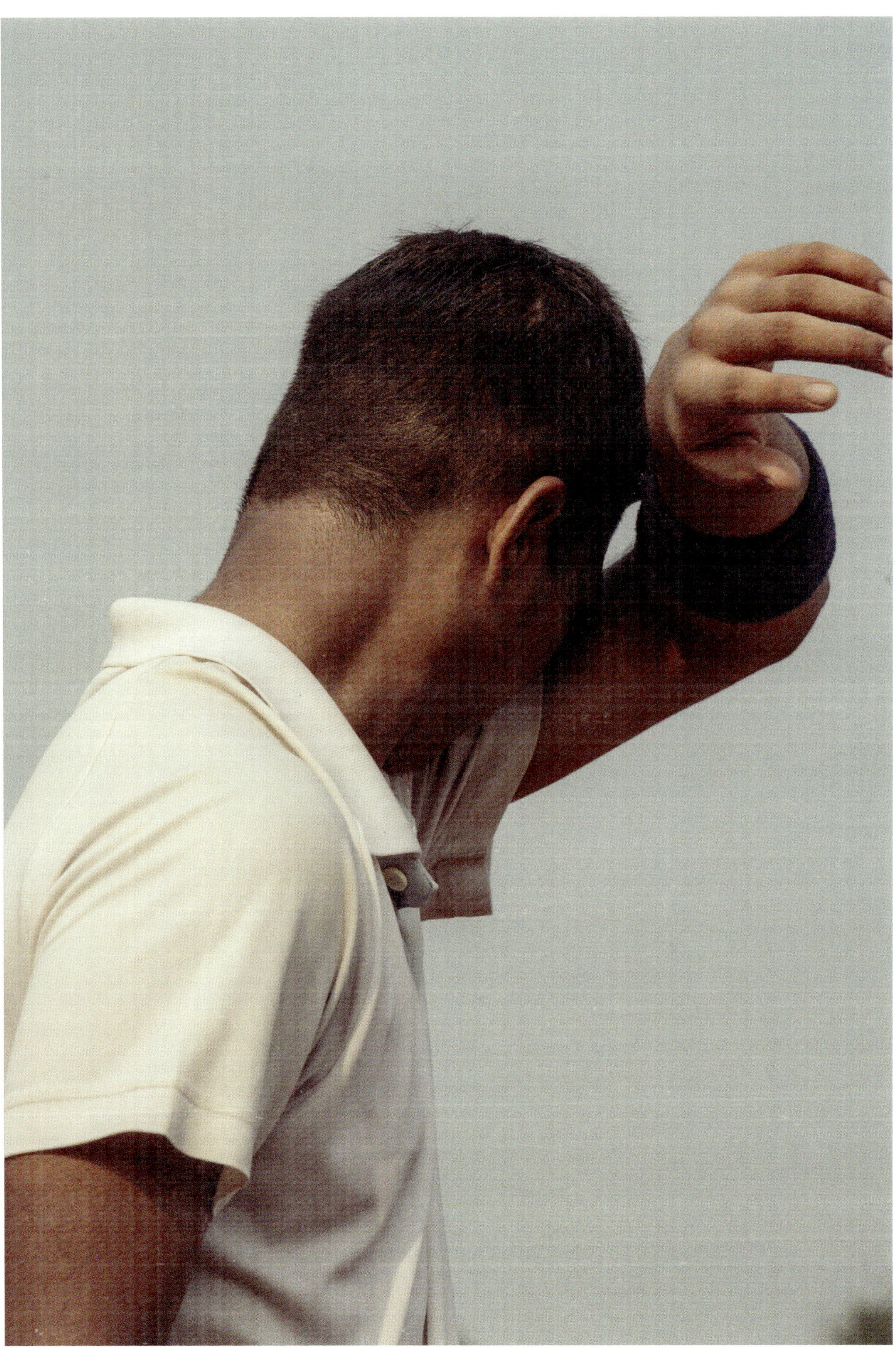

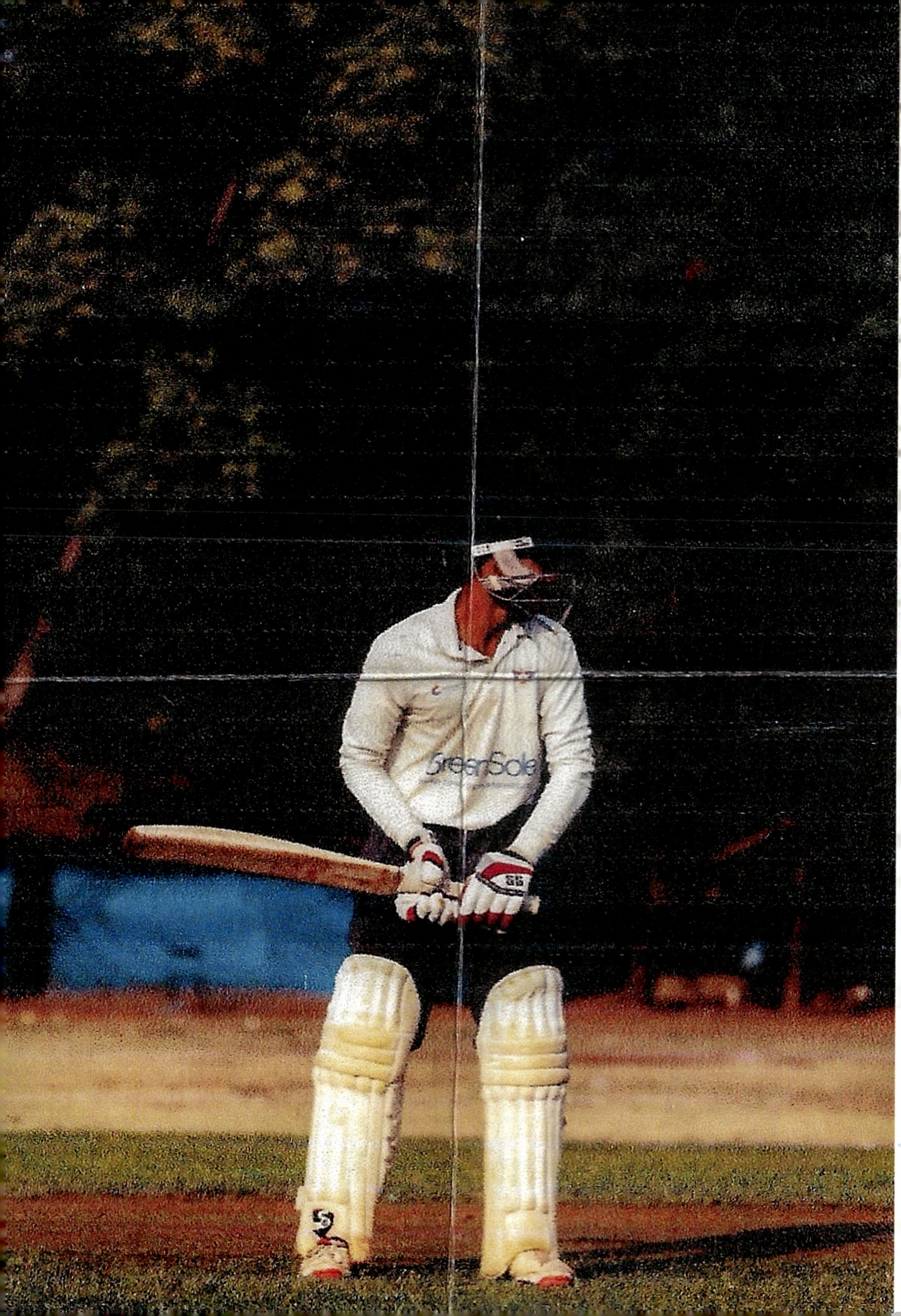
GreenSole

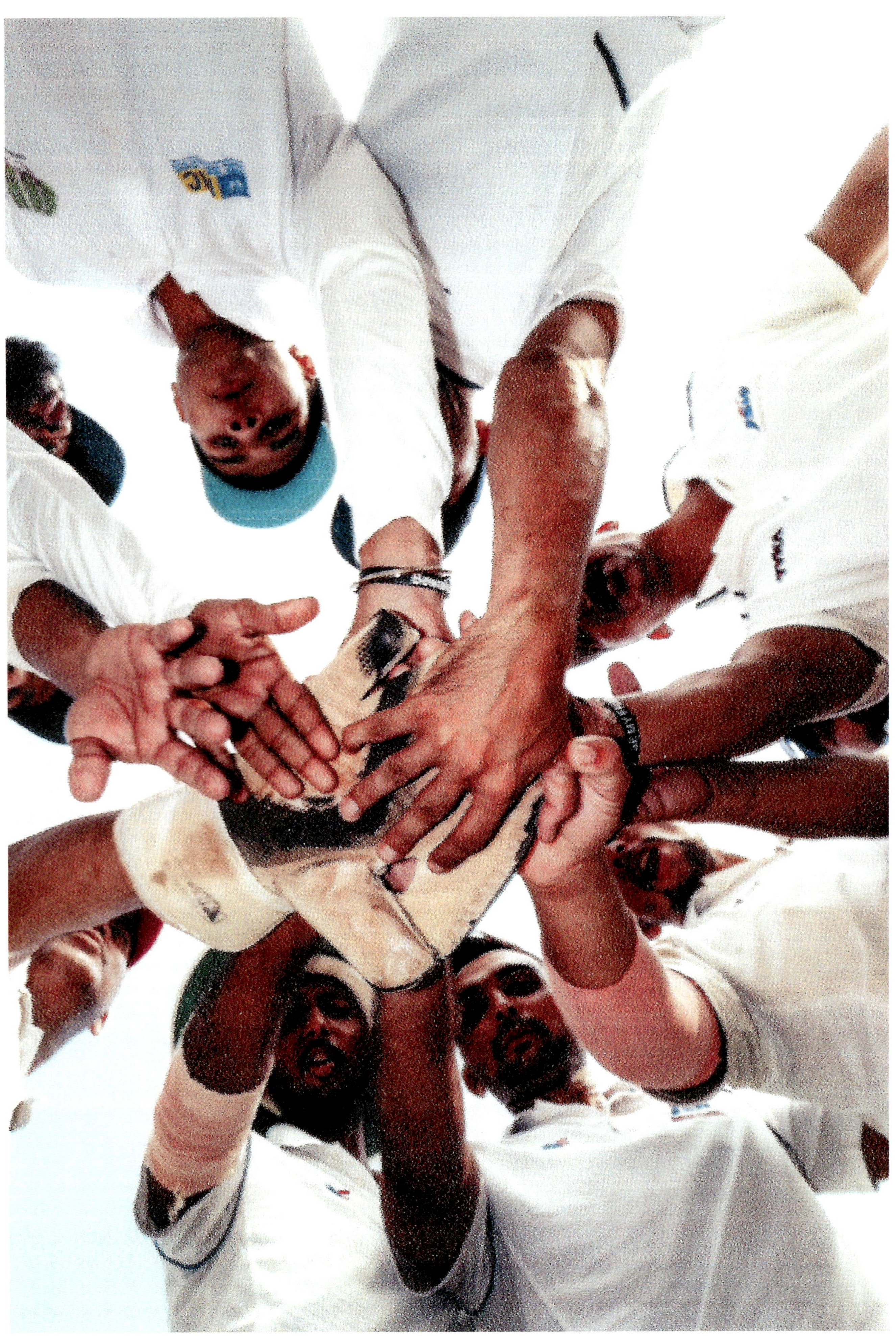

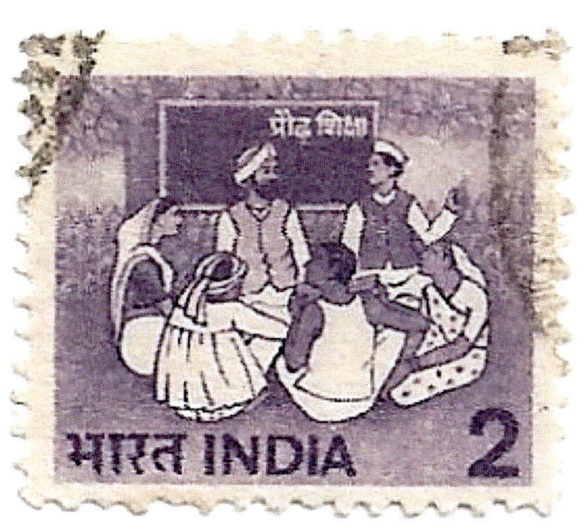
प्रौढ़ शिक्षा
भारत INDIA
2

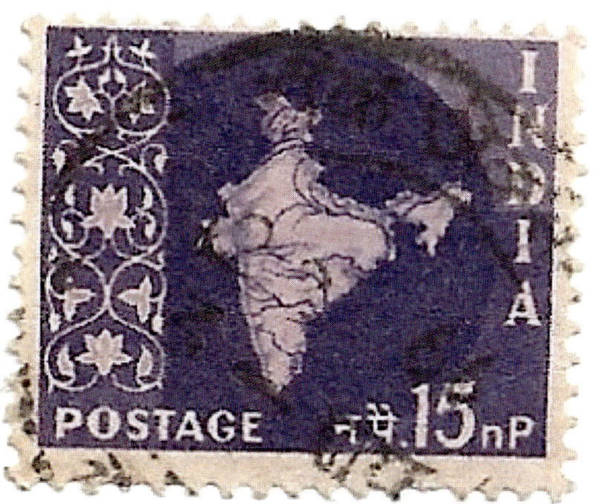
INDIA
POSTAGE
न.पै. 15 nP

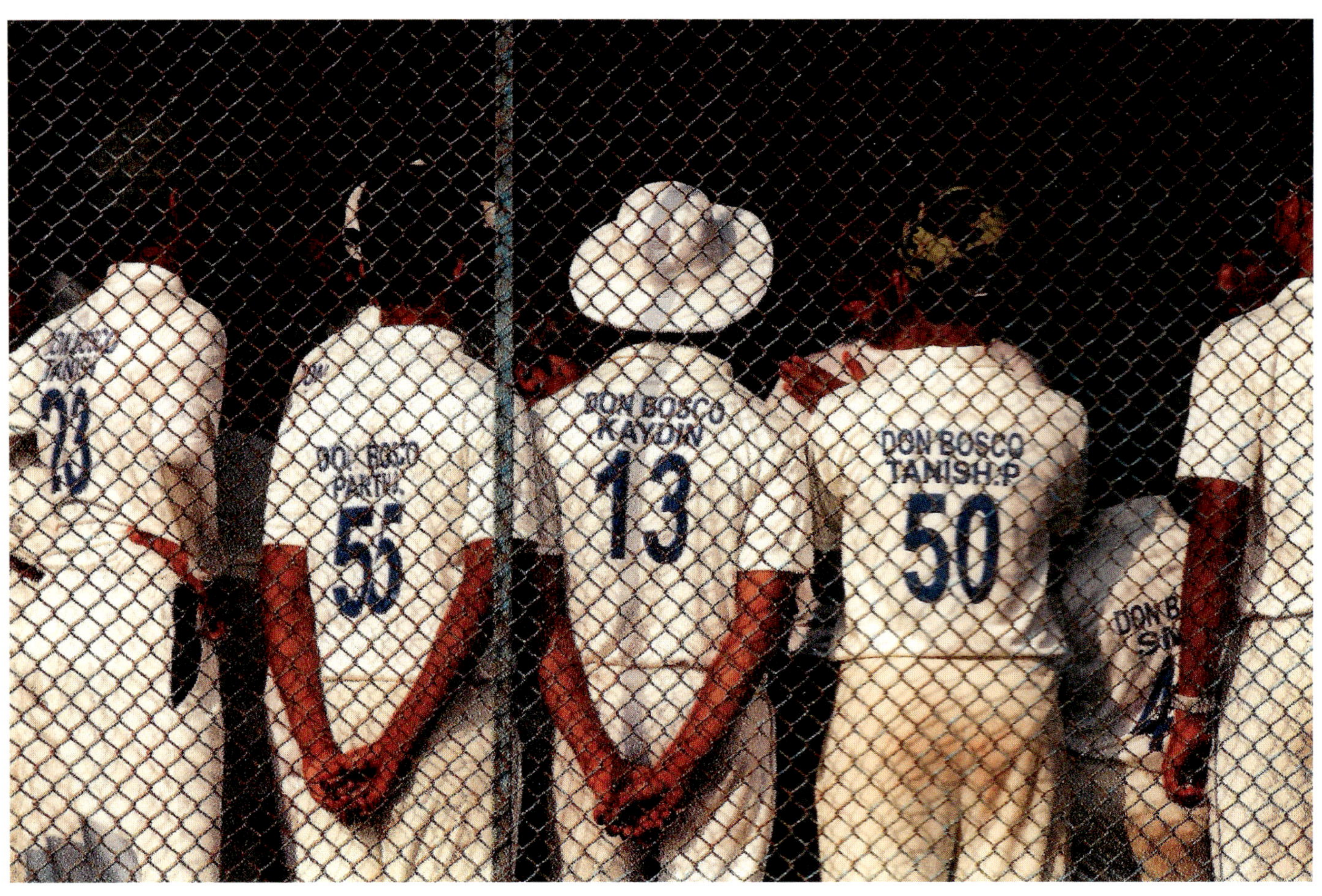
55
DON BOSCO
KAYDIN
13
DON BOSCO
TANISH.P
50

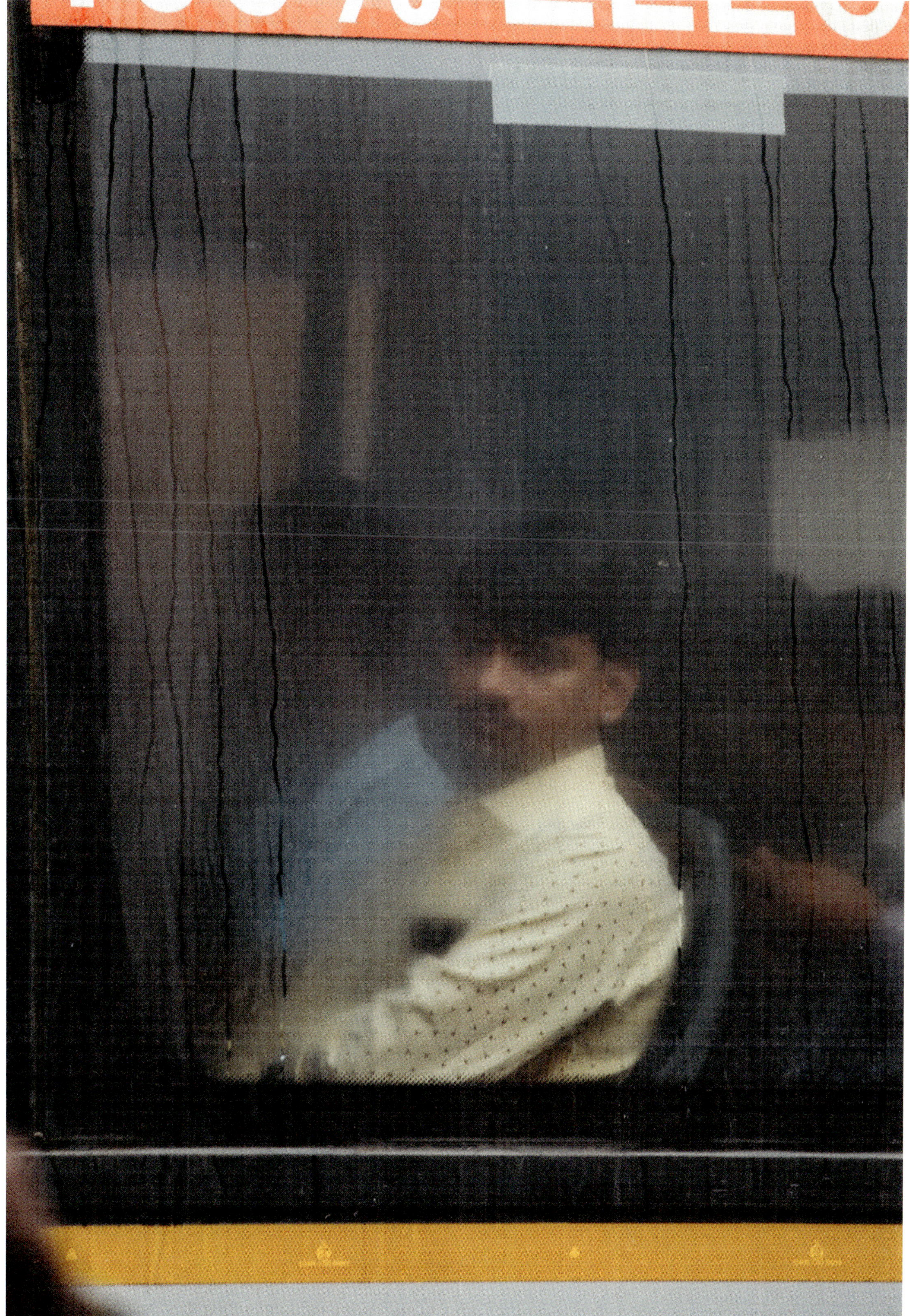

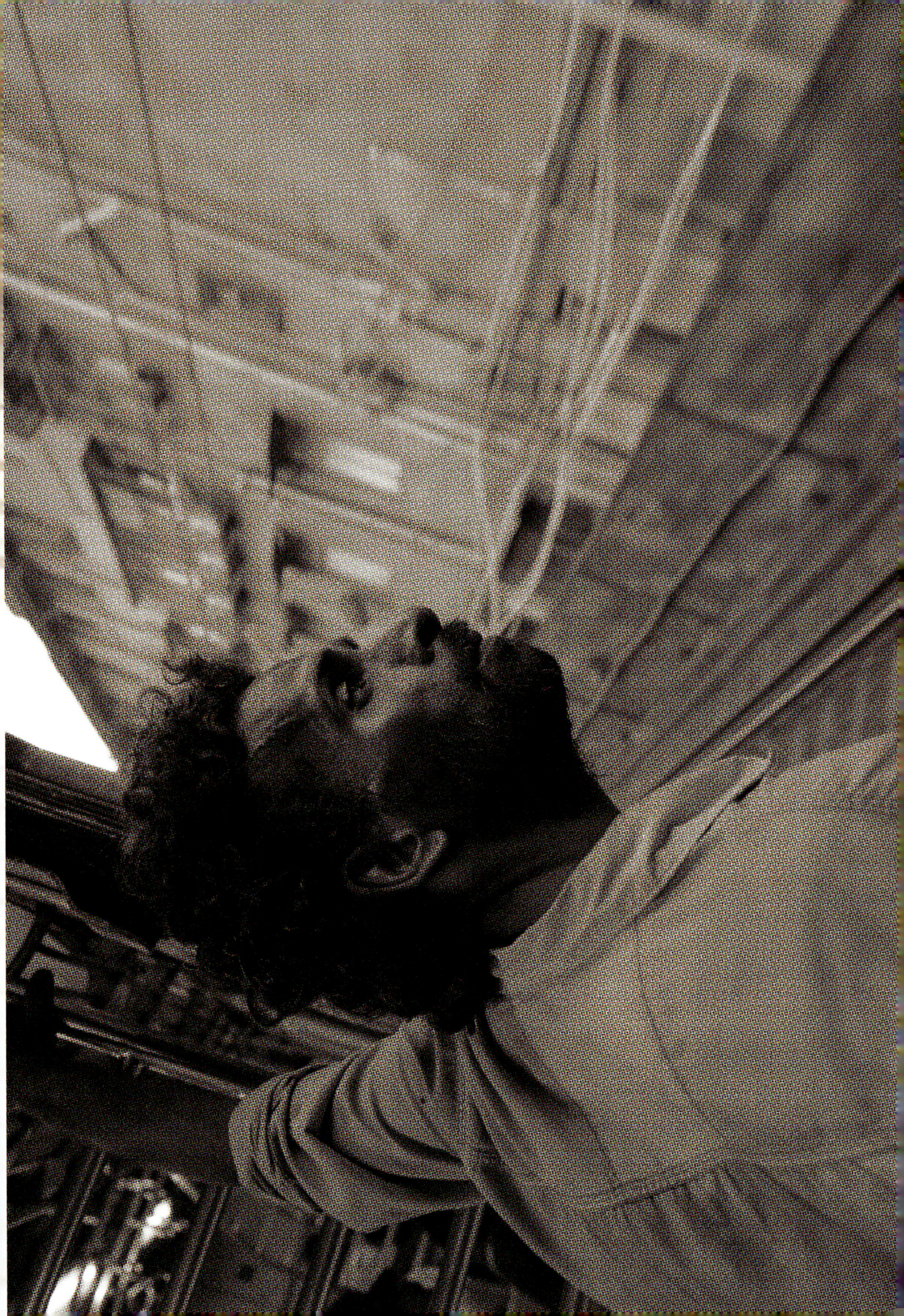

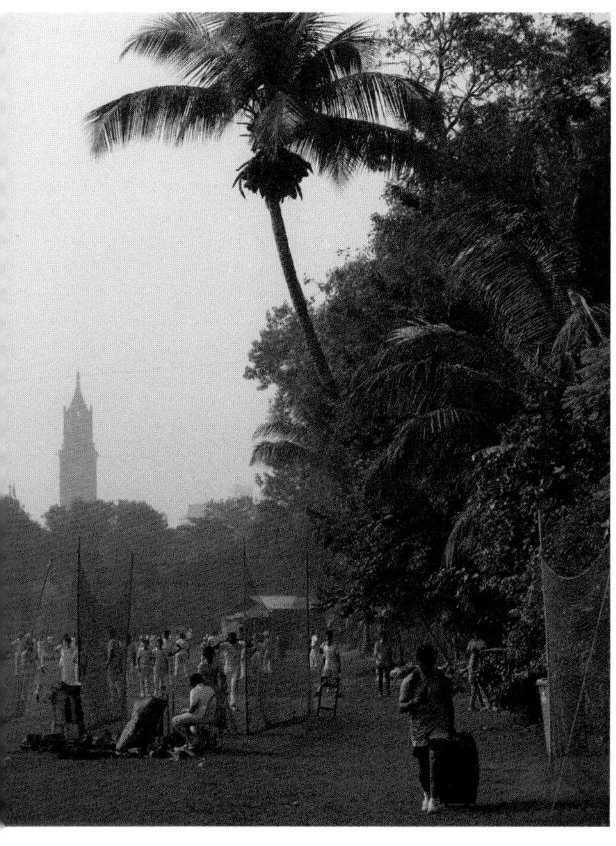
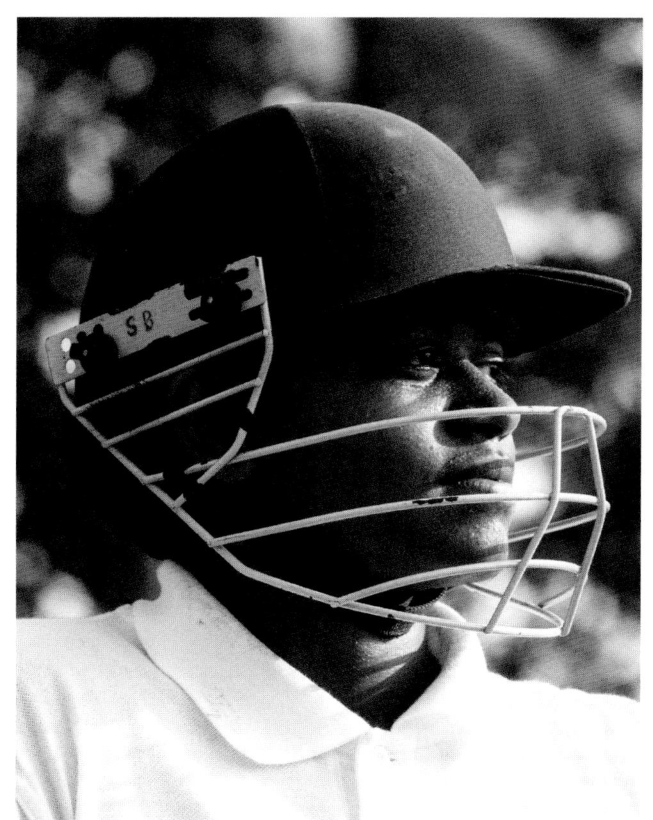

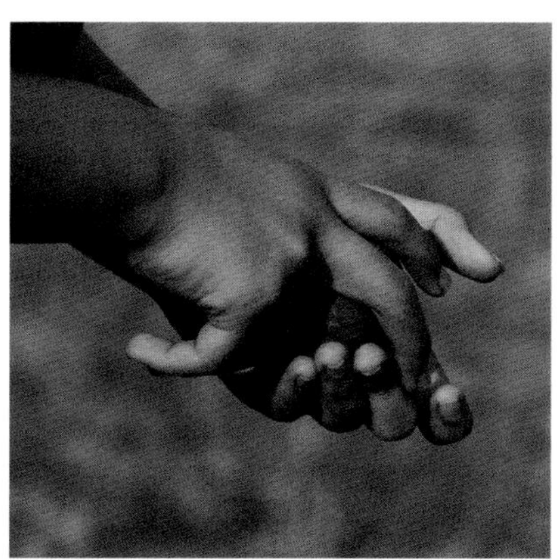
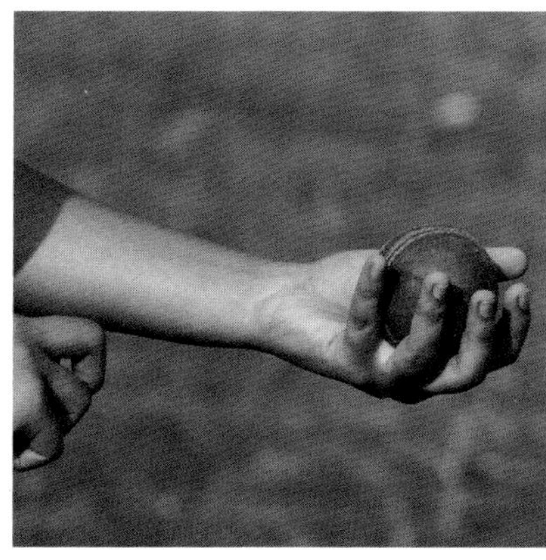
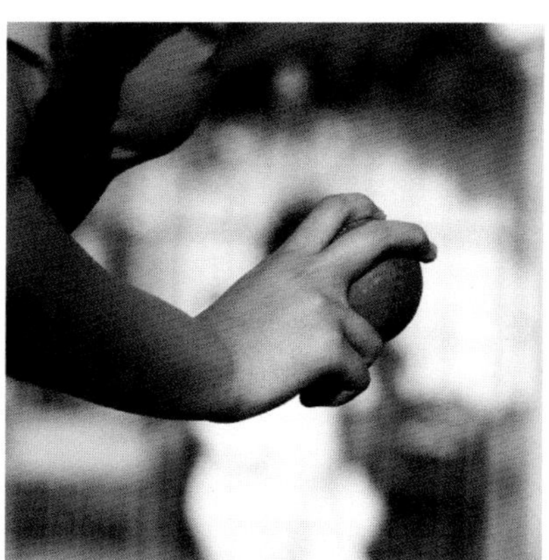
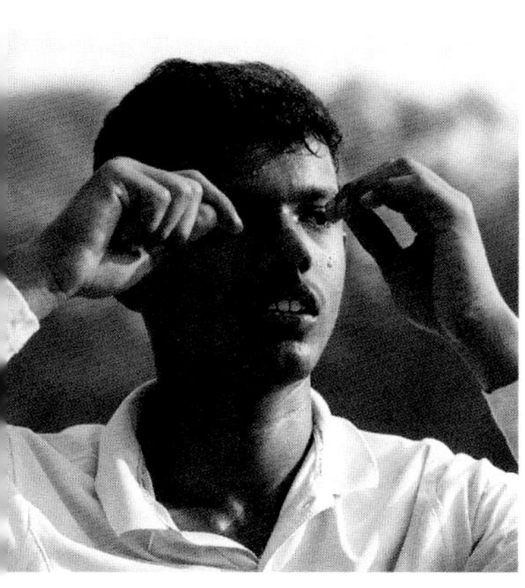
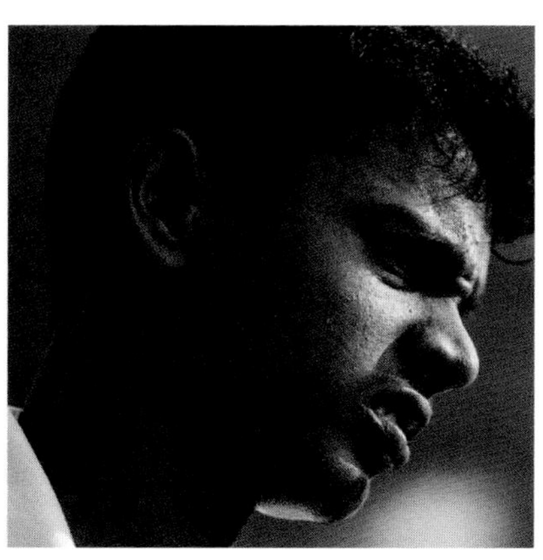

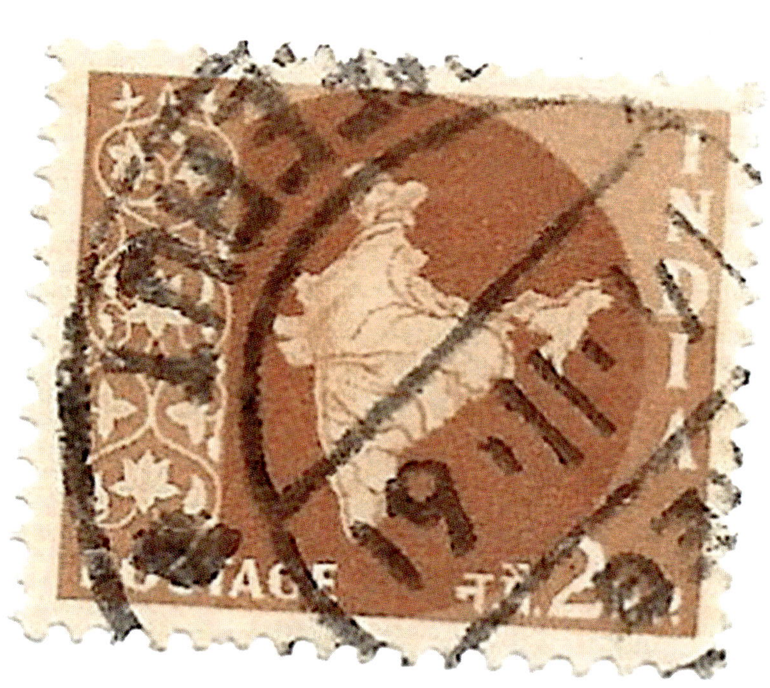
INDIA
POSTAGE

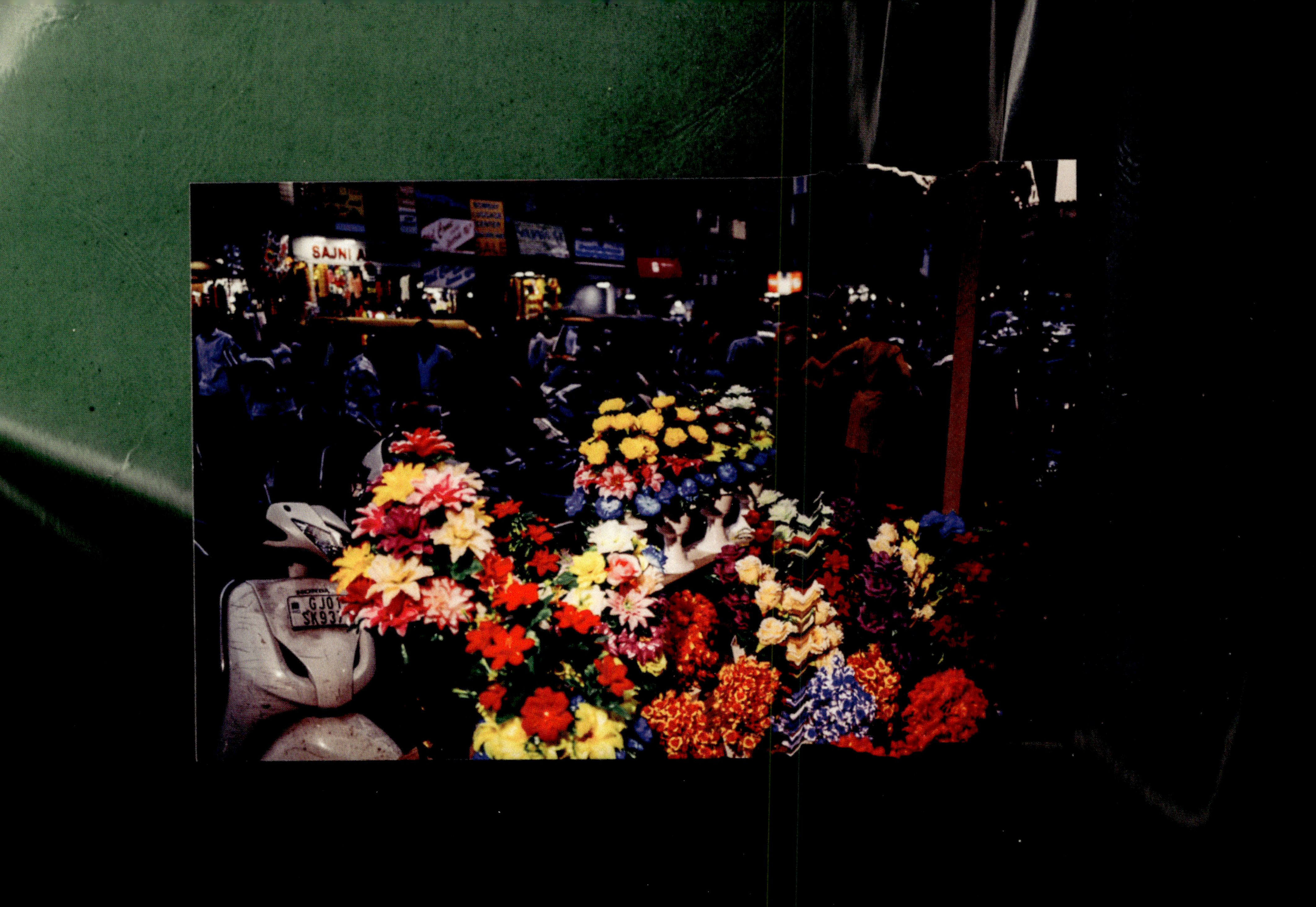
SAJNI

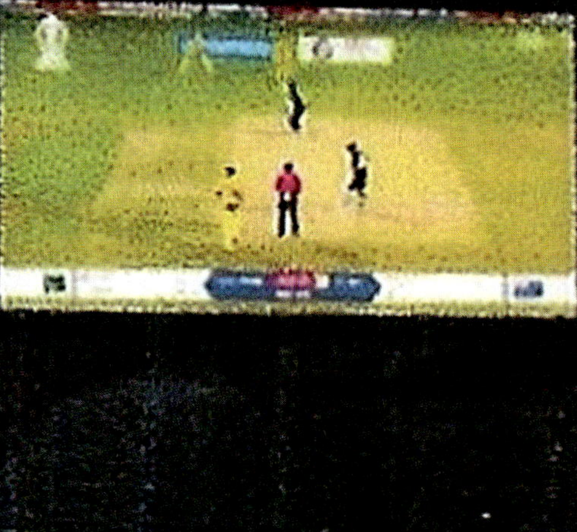

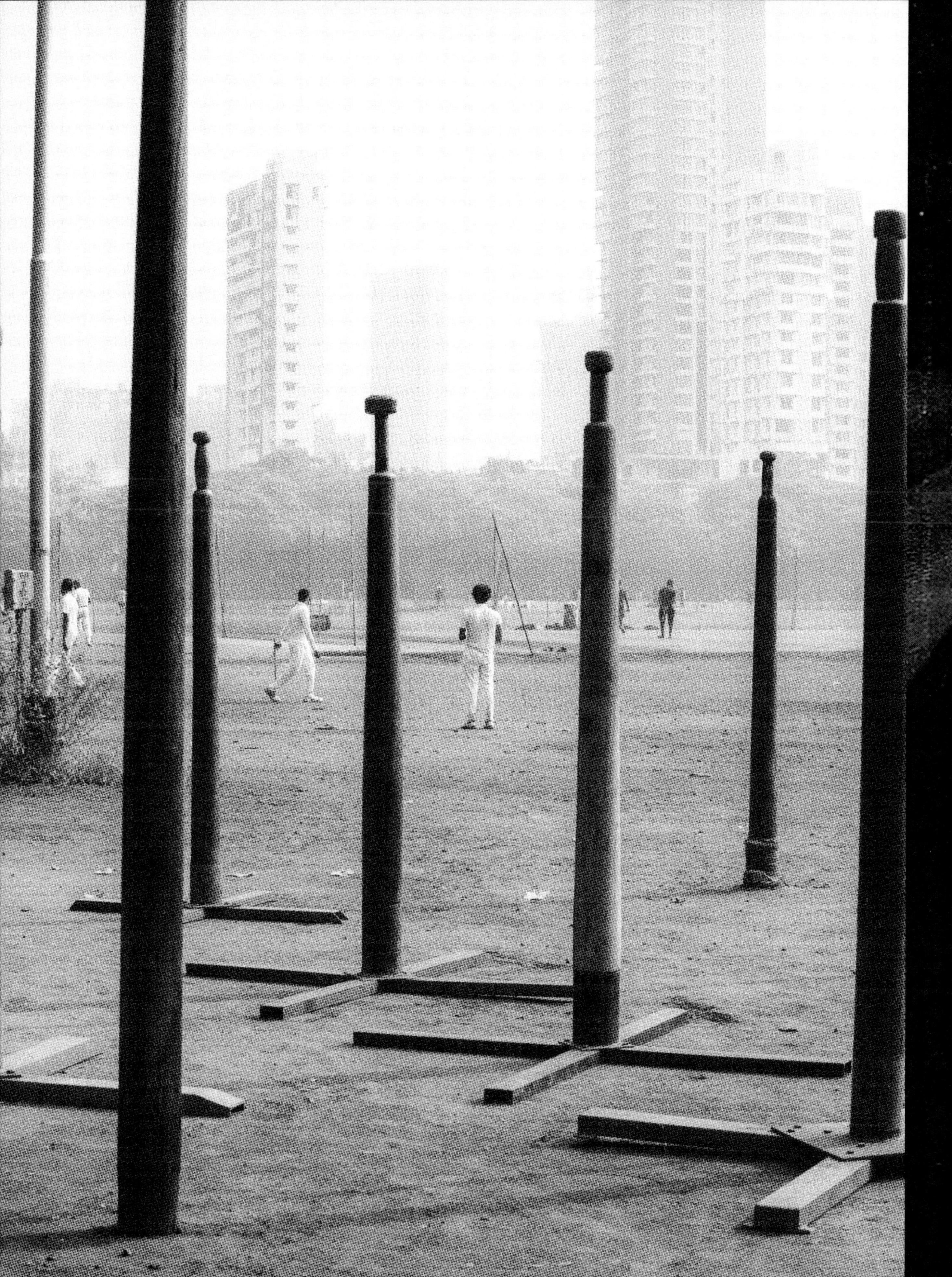

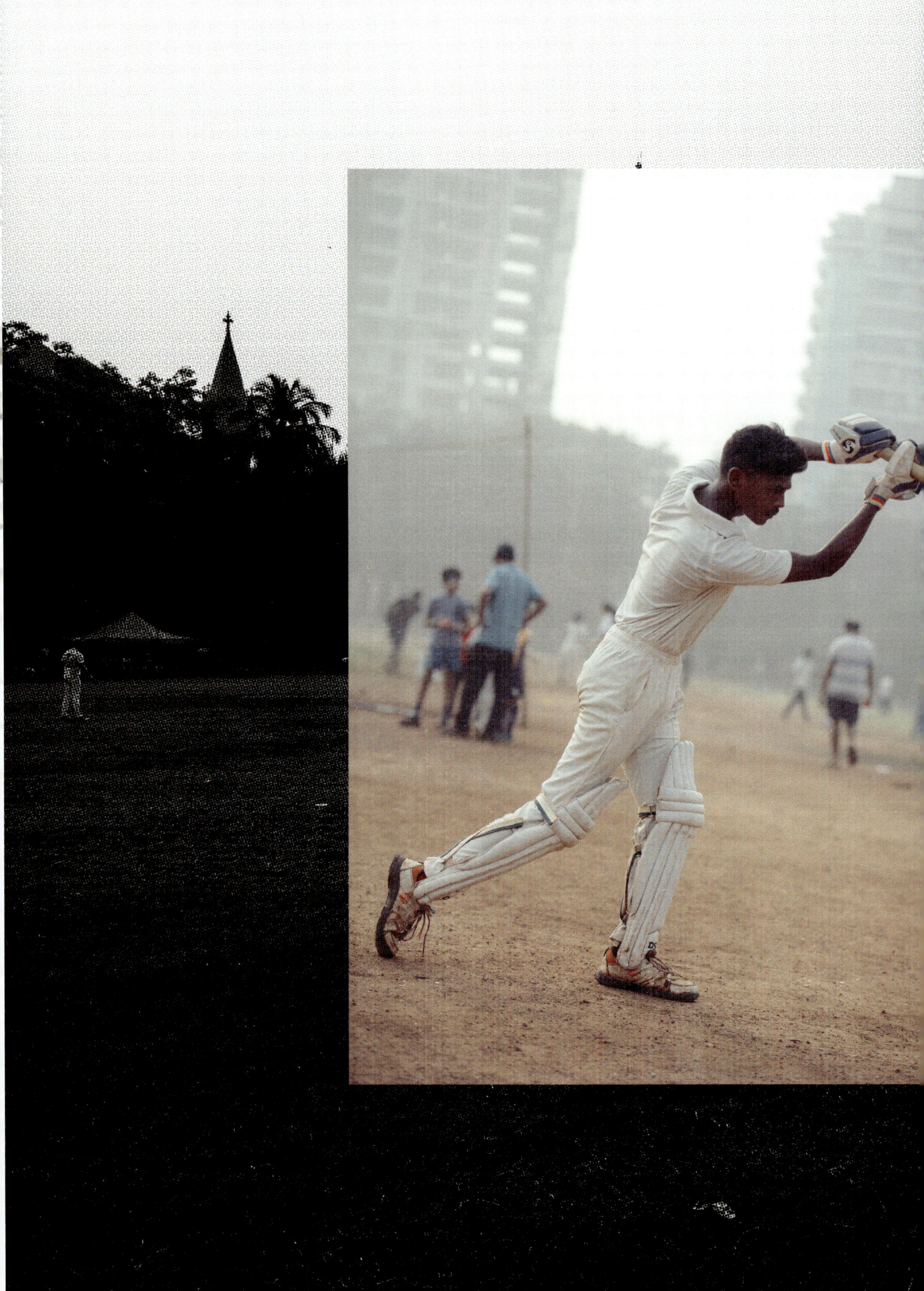

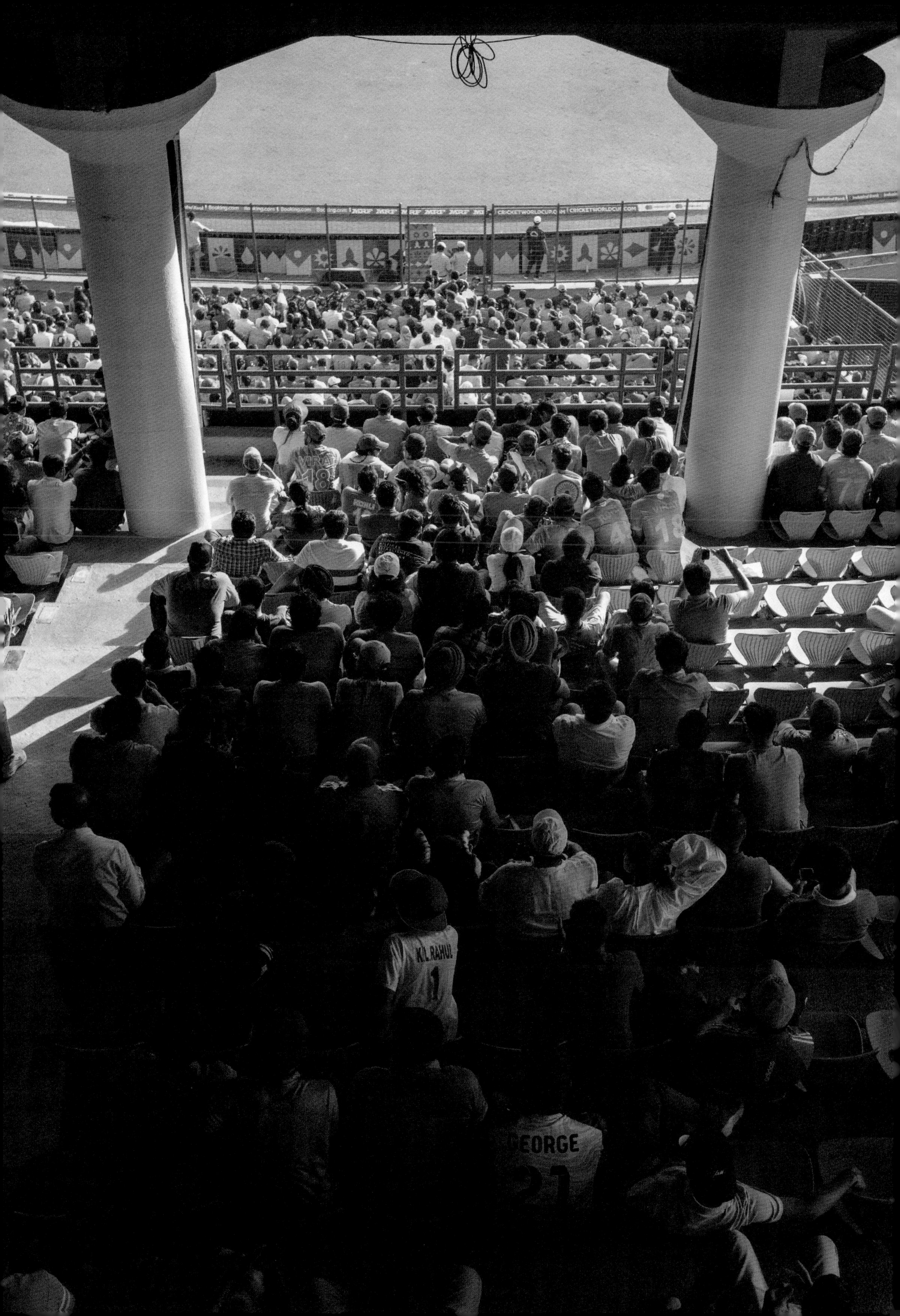
MRF
K.L.RAHUL
1
GEORGE

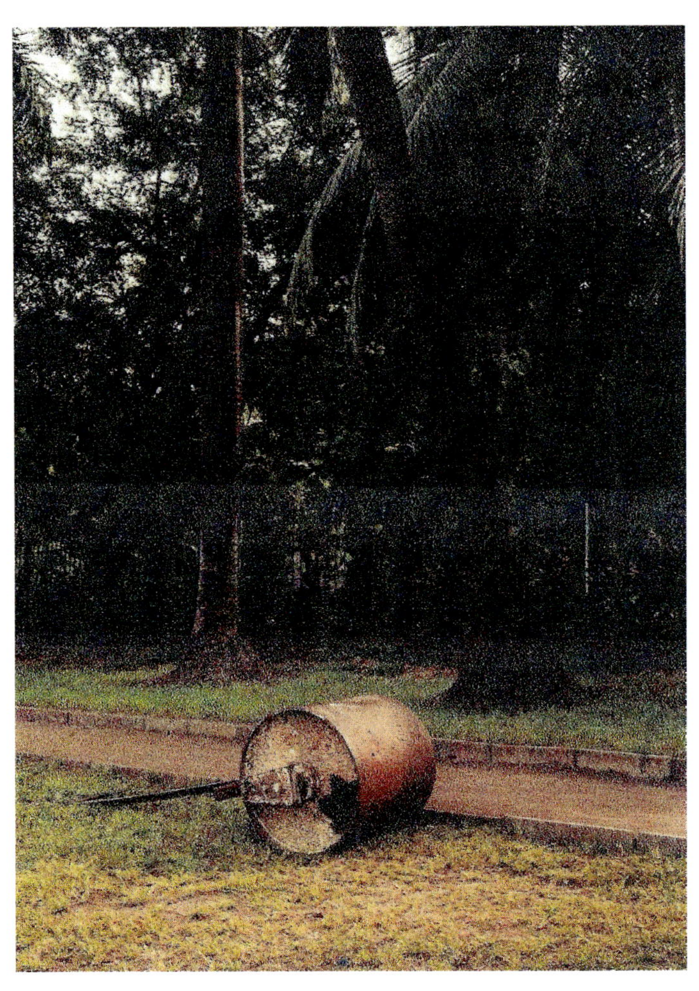

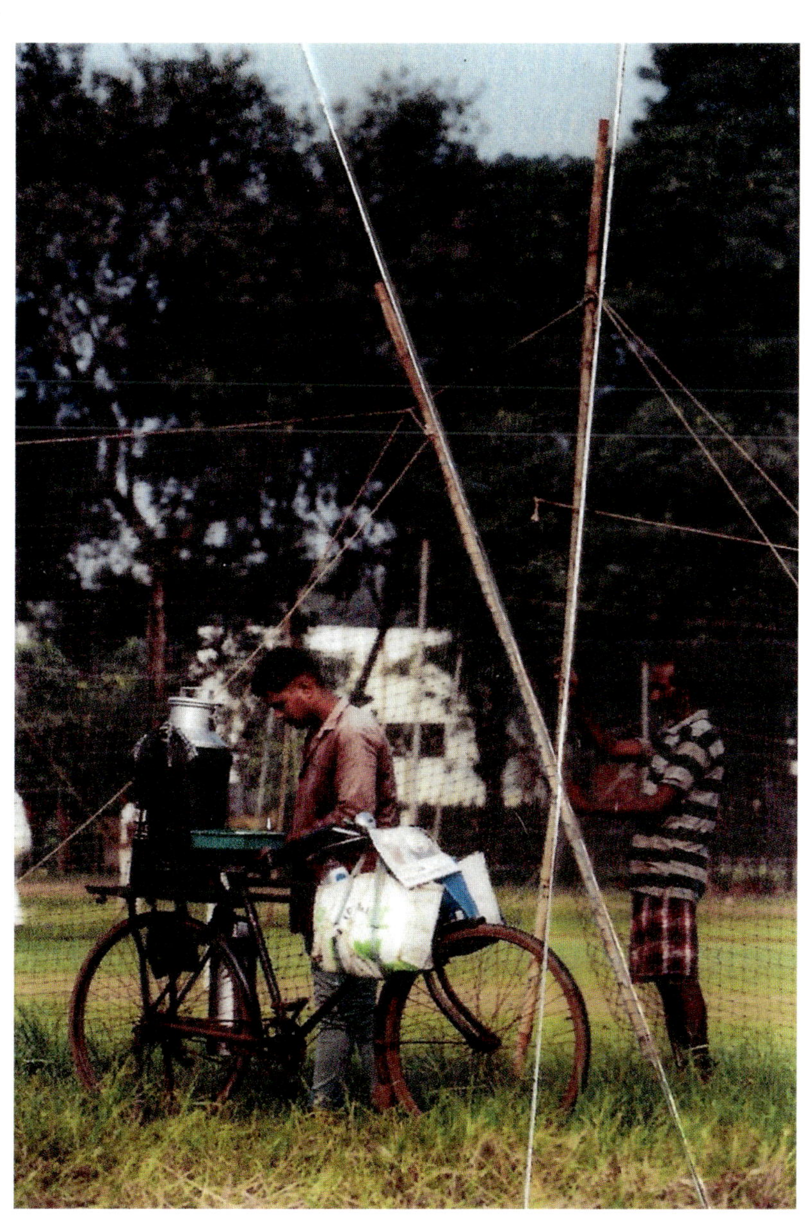

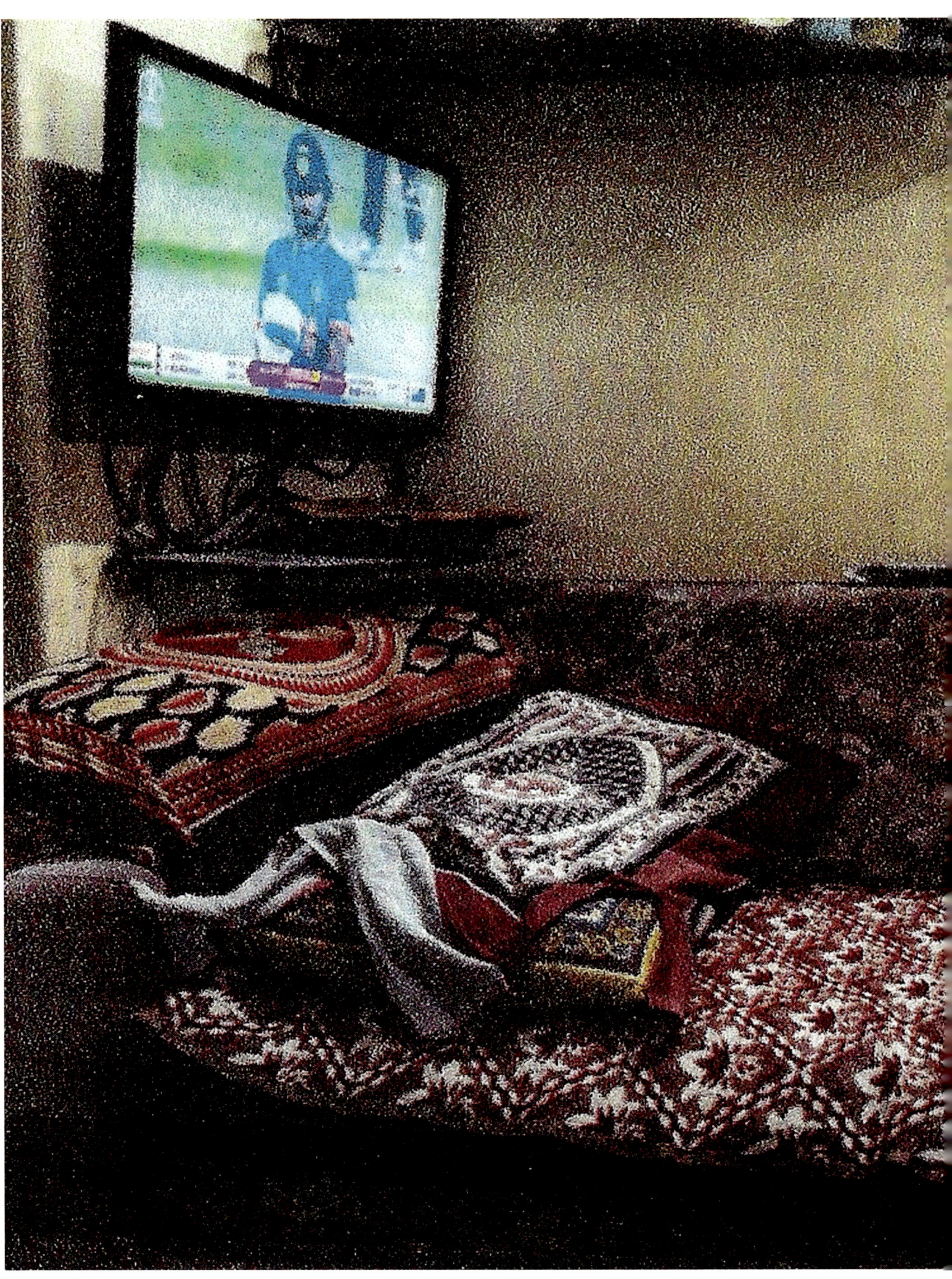

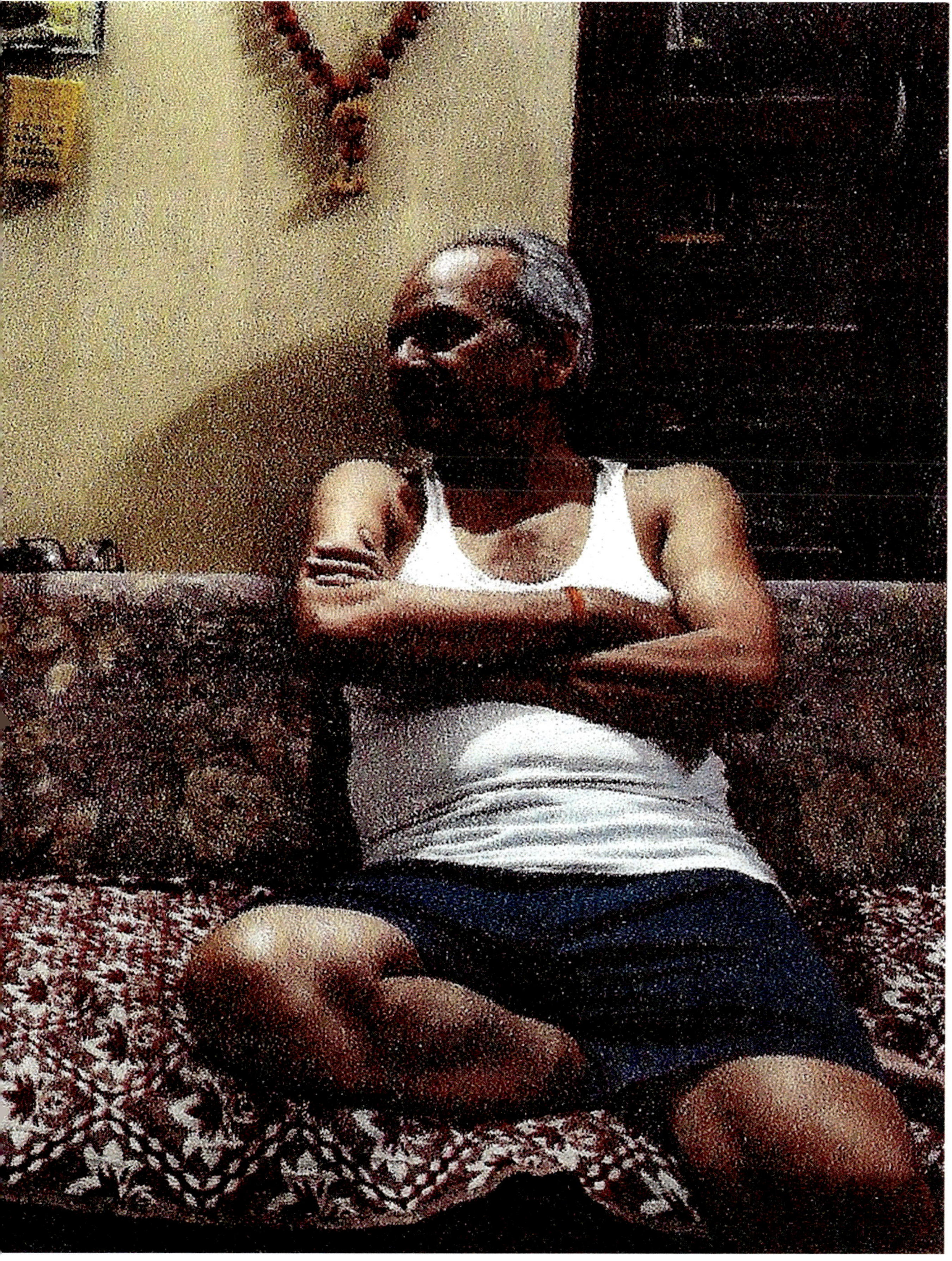

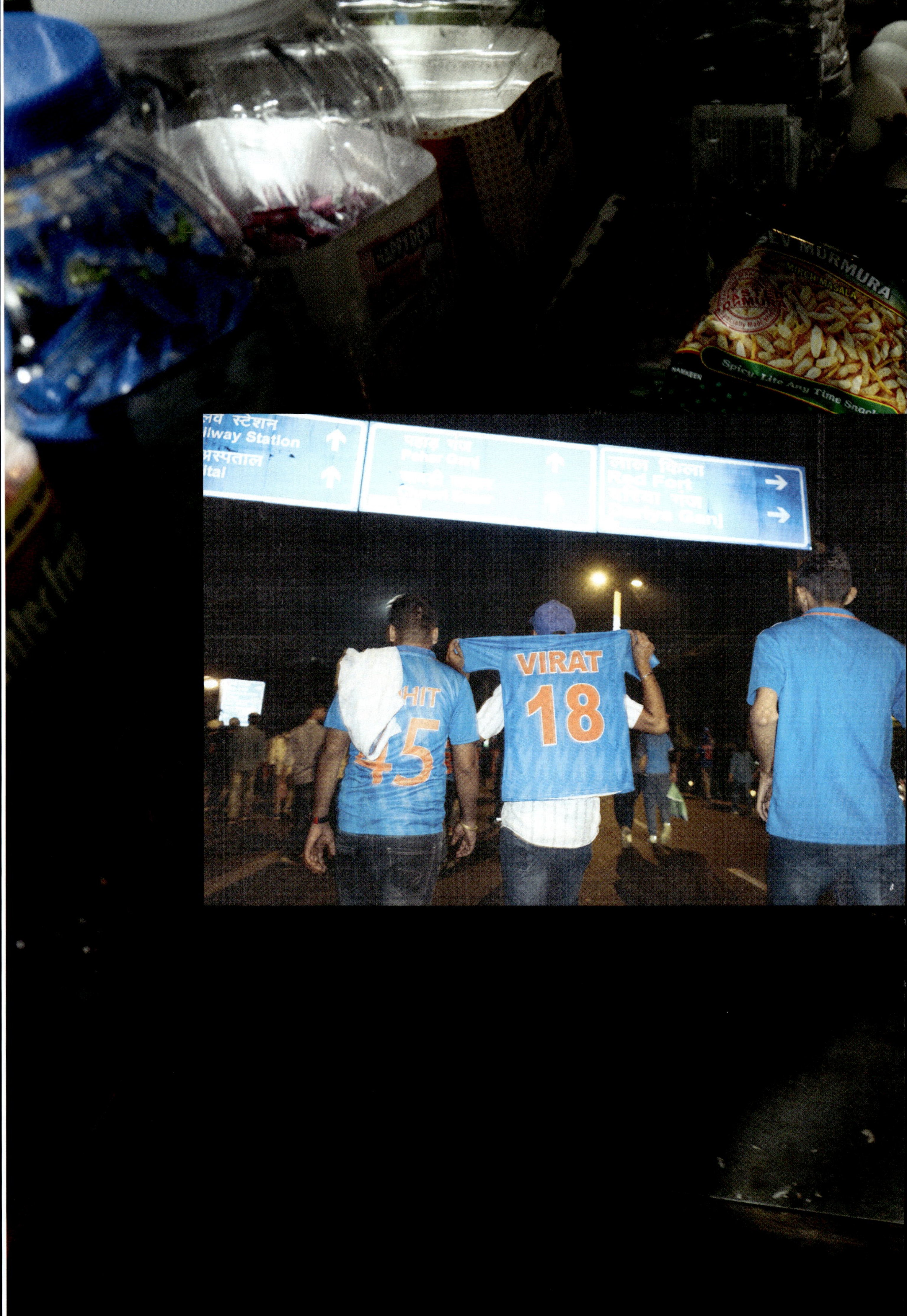
SEV MURMURA
MIRCH MASALA
लाल किला
Red Fort
VIRAT
18
45

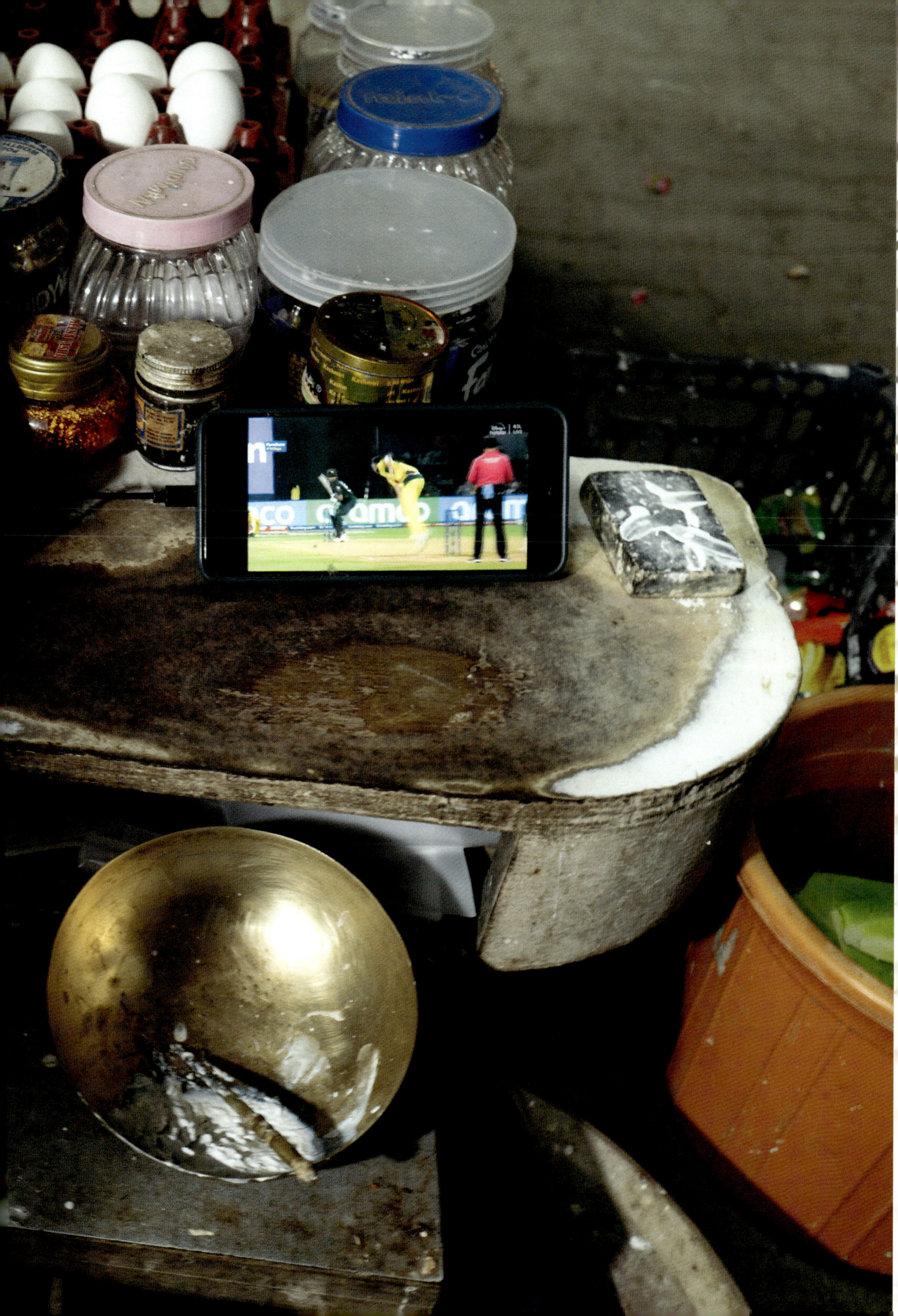

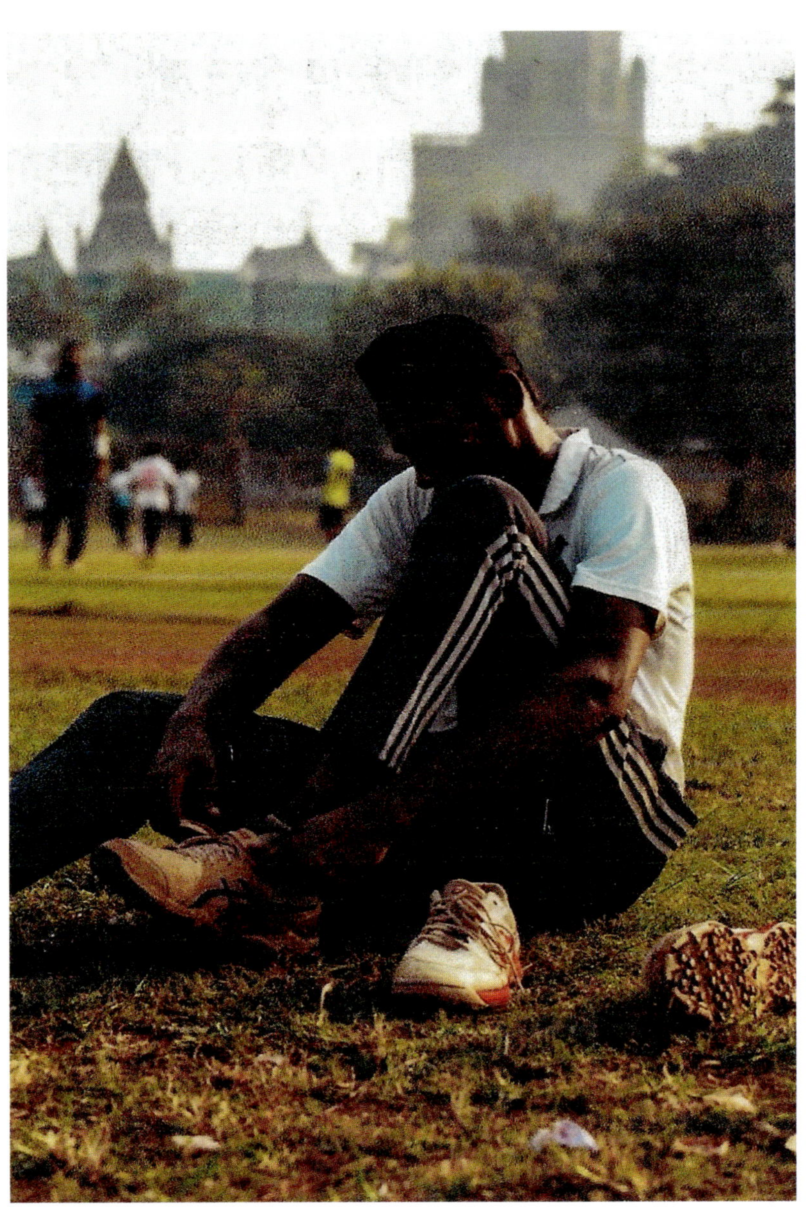

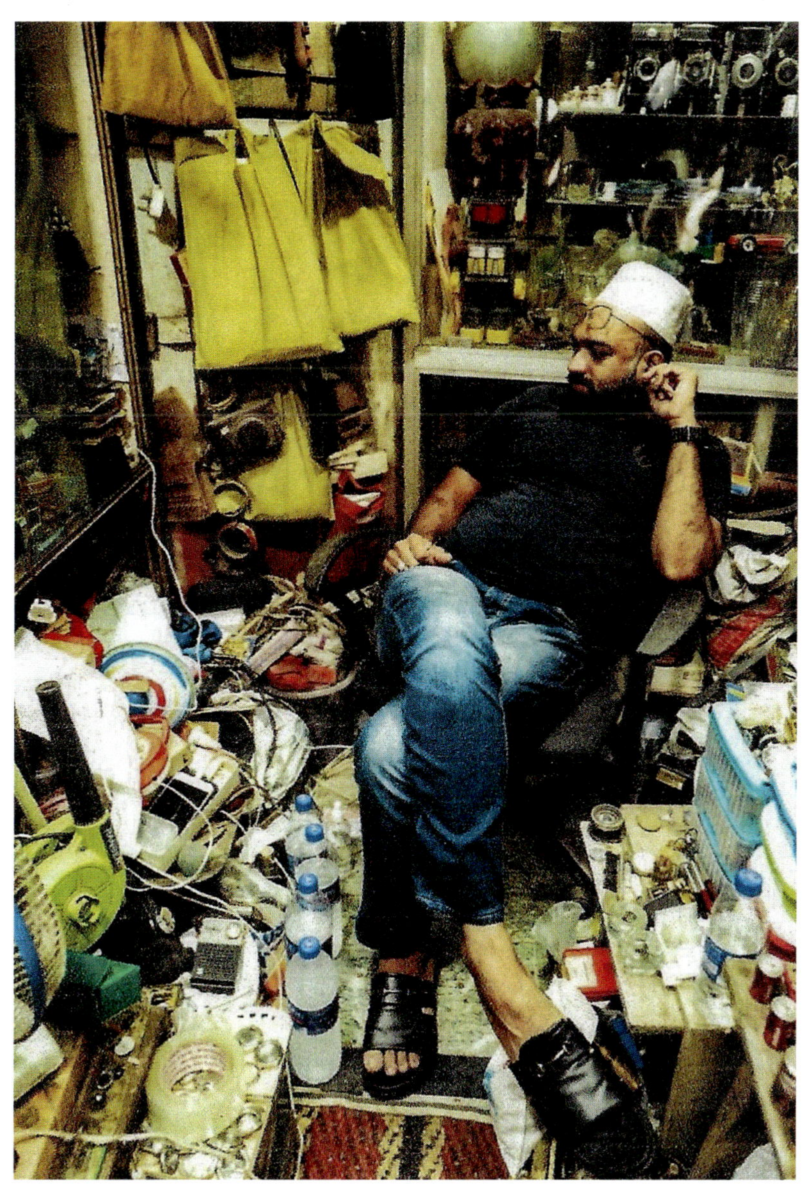

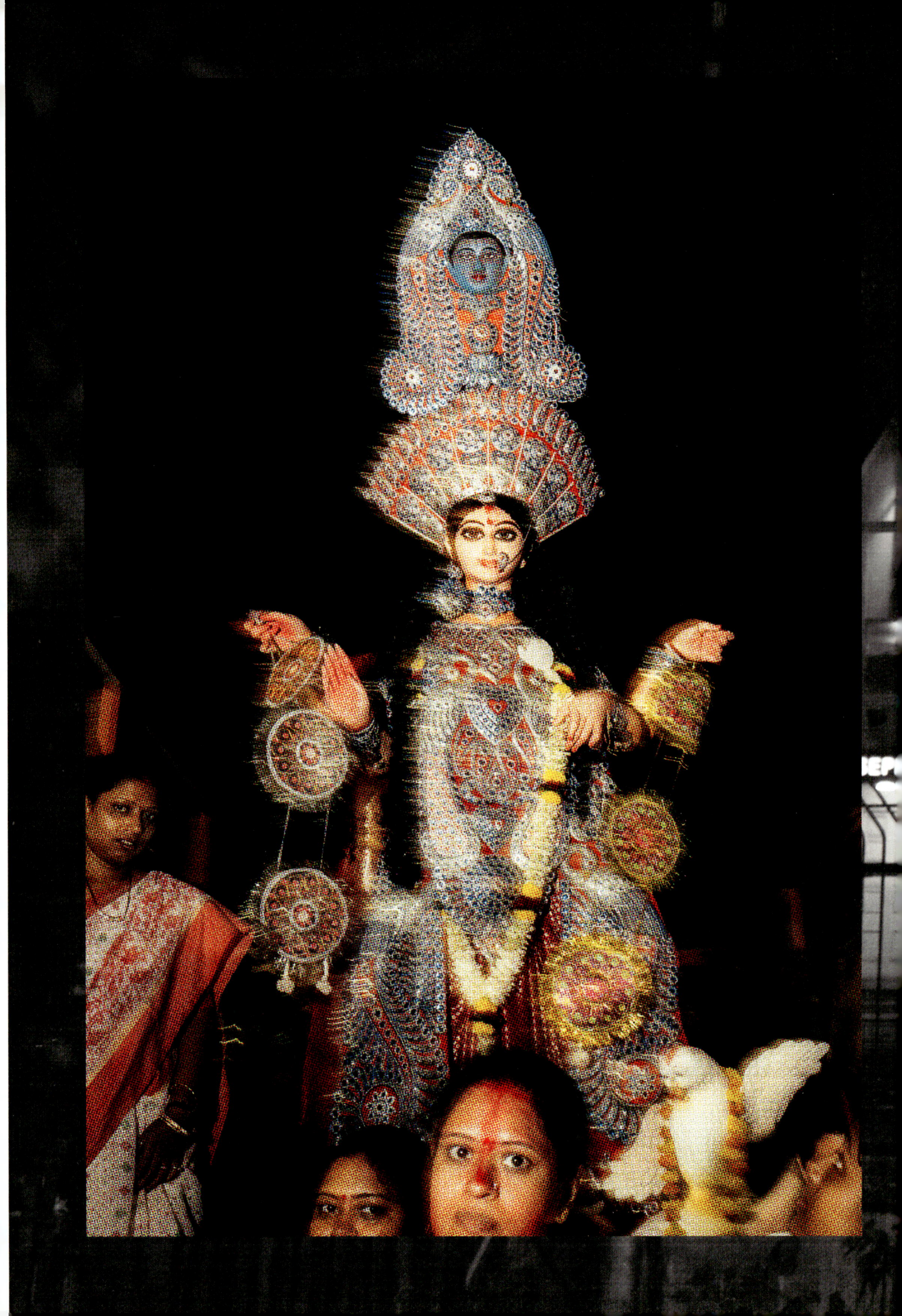

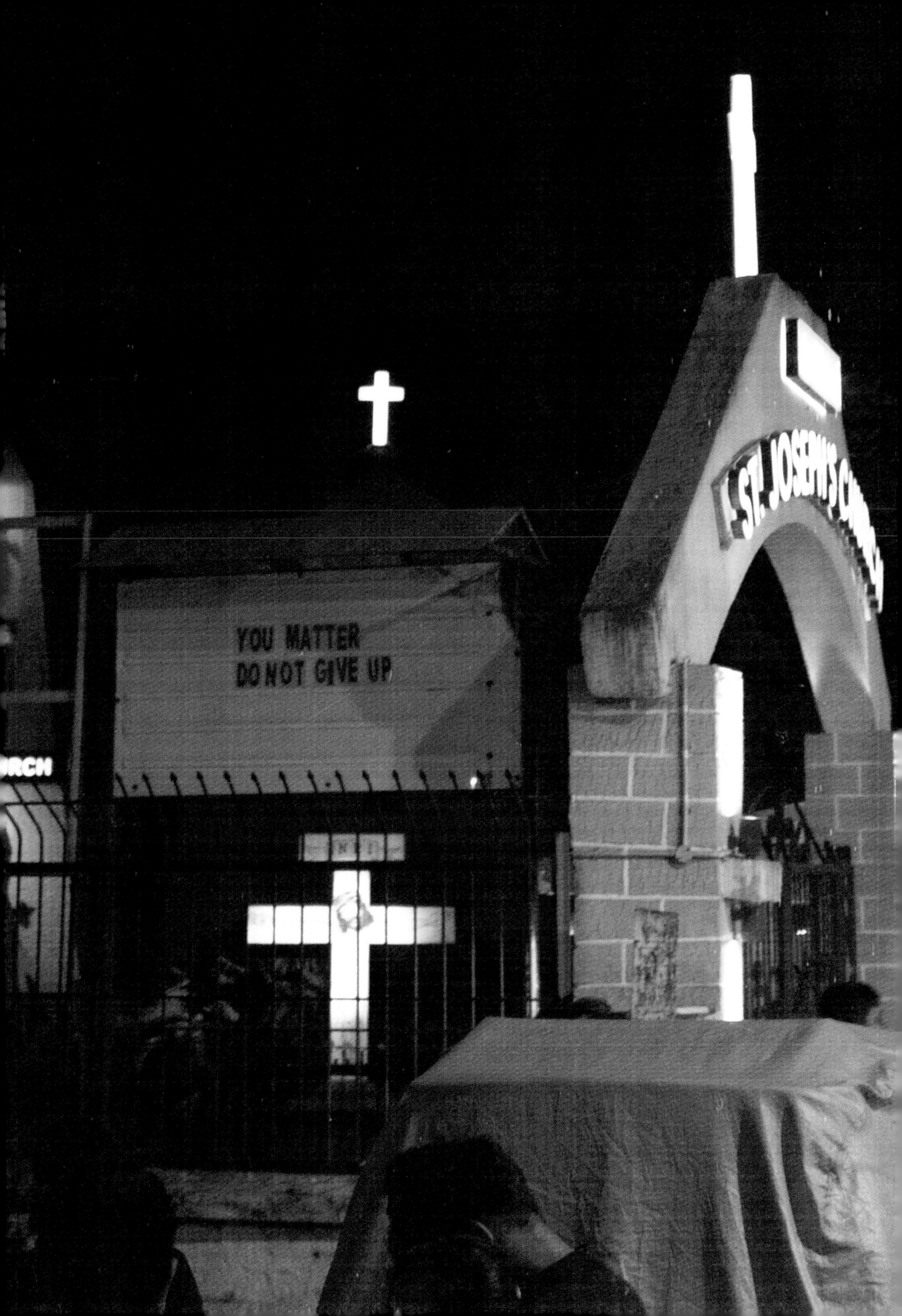

YOU MATTER
DONOT GIVE UP

ST. JOSEPH'S

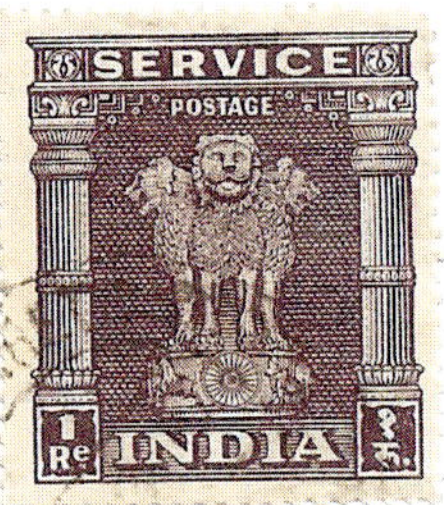
SERVICE
POSTAGE
1 Re
INDIA